THE PHILOSOPHY OF BENEDETTO CROCE

The Philosophy of
BENEDETTO CROCE

An Introduction

ANGELO A. DE GENNARO

Loyola University of Los Angeles

PHILOSOPHICAL LIBRARY

New York

© Copyright, 1961,

by Philosophical Library, Inc.

15 East 40th Street, New York

Library of Congress Catalog Card No. 61-12620

Printed in the United States of America

PREFACE

Benedetto Croce is one of those men who belong to the marvellous period of the first half of twentieth century Italy: a period which presents the minds of Gentile, Rensi, Sturzo, Tilgher and Salvemini. Croce is well known in the world but it seems that this profound thinker has only received occasional notice in the United States.

It is the main purpose of this book to make American scholars more aware of the thought of a man who certainly does not deserve a humble place in a nation which is bound to exercise a great influence upon the minds and hearts of men.

American scholars can justly refute Croce's metaphysics, but no man can reject the message of liberty that one finds in Benedetto Croce. Croce himself often praised American dynamism, the political sagacity of Jefferson and Lincoln and especially in his late years he felt the great importance of the political and cultural life of the American people. In Dante's words "amor, ch'a nullo amato amar perdona."

A.A.D.G.

CONTENTS

I

PRESTIGE

For the Italians Croce was the intellectual leader during his lifetime. Every Italian sensed that during the twentieth century a new spirit of the Italian Renaissance had been born on the Italian soil. Every Italian began to call him "maestro," universal man, the great Croce, the honor of Italian letters, the new Erasmus, the great benefactor. Orazio Raimondo says: "Essentially Croce is a critic whom we young men love for the many good things that we have learned from him and also for the things that he has taught us to understand, giving us a directive and a method that we have never found in the schools which have a musty taste. From him we have learned that to study is not to gather ideas and facts as if they were bottles in a cellar; that the brain is not a vase into which one pours others' ideas; that education is not a pedantic stuffing." [1] The writer concludes: "Truly Croce is one of the greatest benefactors of Italy. We who have drunk at the clear fountain of his teaching revere and love him." [2]

Many Italian and foreign intellectuals frequently made their cultural pilgrimage to the city of Naples. They wanted to converse with Croce, to listen to his voice, to prove the sensation that one feels upon finding himself before a man of genius. Even high school students went to his palace as if compelled by a superior force, the force that Plato calls *enthusiasmos*.

Every day Croce received letters from the United States, South America, Germany, England, Sweden and France, now asking advice on the international situation, now on a cultural problem, be it aesthetic or philosophical, literary or historical.

Never since Galilei had an Italian aroused such world interest. Neither Parini, nor Leopardi, nor Foscolo had the world popularity of Goethe, Shelley and Flaubert; neither Galluppi, nor Rosmini, nor Gioberti had the international fame of Kant, Fichte and Hegel; neither Muratori, nor Balbo, nor Cuoco had the cosmopolitan audience of Gibbon, Mommsen and Michelet.

Young authors often sent him their manuscripts hoping to receive some encouragement; famous writers, their books hoping to receive a kind review; the university professors who at first had considered him an amateur were now paying attention to his voice; the Italian government appointed him senator of the kingdom; the Neapolitan booksellers respectfully waited for his daily visits; the university students eagerly waited for the next issue of his *Critica*. Thus De Ruggiero recalls this enthusiasm for Croce. "It was the time when we young college or university students were waiting for the next issue of the *Critica* like children who wait for the sweets after a boring and interminable dinner. Our souls, desirous of life, oppressed by the jumble of college or university books,

were electrified at that life that was already mature
but nevertheless young and fresh. There was a mixture of great and small feelings, of noble and gossipy
feelings in our attraction toward the *Critica*. . . .
Among these complications of good and bad feelings
Croce's figure assumed the aspect of a god who
had come to redeem us from the mortifications of
school." [3]

His books were translated into many languages,
and his *Filosofia della pratica* was even translated into
Japanese. In his books Croce speaks with the authority of a man who has an international public, of
a man who rules in the *respublica litterarum*. The
same Mussolini who had great contempt for liberals
recognized in him a strong cultural force. Without
doubt this glory was the result of many factors. During the Fascist regime Croce was one of the few
Italians who kept alive the flame of Italian liberty,
that liberty which inspired the hearts and minds of
Cavour and Mazzini and which motivated Foscolo's
immortal *Sepolcri*. For the Italians Croce was the
celebrator of freedom. Croce's concept of freedom is a
metaphysical principle that aims to create the greatest
liberty in human society and that attempts to destroy
tyrannies and oppressions. Croce was a philosopher.
Sorel says: "A few days ago I read Renan's *Essais* and
I came upon a passage inspired by Ferrari's *Rivo-
luzioni d'Italia*: what sad reflections upon the destiny
of Italy! But in reading certain newspapers and re-
views that are published today in Italy and, above all,
in following its recent intellectual movement initiated
by Benedetto Croce, whom the future will regard as
the greatest thinker of our times, I began to have
confidence. The country which justly prides itself on
having given birth to the greatest geniuses of man-

kind and which has seriously been compromised by
the levity of its leading classes, will be saved by the
new generation. I am firmly convinced." [4] Croce was
a great erudite or "cultural giant." [5] He had thou-
sands of books in his personal library: books on history, philosophy, literature, linguistics, painting,
architecture, economics and politics. His close friends
saw him always working twelve hours a day. He was
the Neapolitan Wagner. "What a tortured life lived
Faust in the effort of finding the realm of truth and
life! What a delicious life lived his servant Wagner
who spent the winter nights on books, papers: happiness was all over his face and if he was running
through a venerable parchment it seemed to him that
the whole of heaven was descending on him! When I
amorously analyzed and interpreted that stupendous
creature of the Goethian genius, a sly censor of mine
observed that I had understood it so well because I
resembled him: a thing that did not displease me because Wagner was one of the rare gentlemen whom
Faust encountered in his adventurous life. Certainly:
I have often enjoyed, and even today I do, those de-
lights of the erudition hunter, of the solver of small
enigmas, of the lover of curiosities." [6] Severe was his
bibliographical scrupulosity. He never quoted any
writer without giving all the necessary details.

Croce's books ranged from Aristotle's *Poetics* to
Hegel's *Encyclopedia,* from Tacitus' *Annals* to Car-
lyle's *Sartor Resartus,* from Homer's *Odyssey* to
Goethe's *Faust,* from Calderón's plays to Marx's *Capital,* from Mariana's *History of Spain* to Milton's *Paradise Lost,* from Kant's works to Berenson's books,
from Spengler's *Decline of the West* to De Rojas'
Celestina, from Livy's works to Menander's comedies,
from Ruskin's *Stones of Venice* to Da Vinci's draw-

ings. Croce also had a deep knowledge of Greek, Latin, German, English, French, Spanish and Portuguese.

But without doubt his most beloved books were those of Vico and De Sanctis, Hegel and Kant, Herbart and Labriola, books to which he always refers in the course of his scholarly life. Among the thinkers' names that of Hegel is the most frequently quoted, and Hegel's name never appears without the adjective "grande" or the noun "genio." Croce's appreciation for Hegel takes a peculiar color. In it one finds a fantastic, friendly, moving tone. Hegel makes Croce's heart tremble, and Croce goes on an imaginary trip to Germany and visits the German professor. " 'What is it?' said Professor Hegel, lifting his head from the big study desk and from the papers in which he was engrossed and interrogating the servant about the knock he had heard. 'A foreigner who wants to know if you will receive him.' " [7] Croce's intense interest in Hegel transforms the German thinker into a living person. Before Croce some other Italian thinkers such as Vera and Bertrando Spaventa had already propagated the thought of the German philosopher. But Croce was the real apostle of Hegel in Italy and Europe.

It is also true that Croce's adversaries accused him of repeating Hegel without adding anything new or original. Croce rejected this accusation with great firmness. Croce reiterated that he had accepted Hegel's "concrete-universal," the solution of the dualism between the positive and the negative, evil and goodness, but he also added the identification of philosophy with historiography, the practical character of the natural sciences and the dualism between rationality and reality not from the historical but from the moral point of view. He also rejected Hegel's

Philosophy of nature, the dualism between Idea and
Nature, the Philosophy of history [8] and the applica-
tion of the dialectical method to the empirical concepts or to the historical collective processes. Then
as now envious scholars (Enriques, Cervesato) tried
to misrepresent Croce's thought. But, Croce defended
himself very well.

Croce's fame was also due to his immense biblio-
philism. Croce loved books in their materiality. For
years, for example, Croce had been looking for a copy
of the very rare *Aesthetica* of Baumgarten, a book
that he had read after borrowing it from a German
library. But Croce wanted to own the book to which
he owed so much of his spiritual life. A few years
went by. One day one of the booksellers who was
aware of Croce's desire let him know that the *Aesthetica* was available at a certain price. Croce hurried
to write that he was accepting the offer, and for a few
days he continually feared that something would happen to prevent the transaction. Finally, the book
arrived and Croce turned it up and down and contemplated it with "joyful satisfaction." In the "joyful
satisfaction" one feels that the Neapolitan thinker is
deeply moved.

We can add that this love for books was an old
one. In the *Contributo alla critica di me stesso* Croce
evokes his childhood and he points out that at the
age of six or seven he had a great affection for books
and that even their odor was pleasant to him. Here
one finds the germ of his future bibliophilistic
activity.

Every human being is born with a certain vocation
that some realize and others do not really fulfill. But
those who successfully carry into effect their calling
really experience it at a very early age. In Leibniz's

words "nous sommes gros de l'avenir." This can be seen in some great historical personalities such as Leopardi and Hannibal. Croce's love for the odor of books is not without significance. In Croce this early love later becomes a true and profound enthusiasm.

II

POSITIVISM AND IDEALISM

Before entering into an analysis of Croce's system it is necessary to place Croce in the historical positivistic atmosphere of the first years of the twentieth century in order to become conscious of his immense philosophical effort. I lack the necessary preparation and talent to portray a historical era. But Croce himself gives us a clear picture of this materialistic age with his continuous reactions against its spirit and manifestations.

Croce attempts to fight the cult of matter with his own metaphysics. Instead of the principle of matter [1] Croce recurs to a principle which was more or less traditional: traditional not in the sense that it already was a part of the heritage of Western culture but in the sense that this same principle was more or less implicit in German idealism. There is nothing so well known as Kant's synthesis *a priori:* with its categories the human mind almost creates reality. One finds the same idea in Fichte, a thinker who holds that the autonomous *Ichheit* creates the world.

"Then the Spirit is the Act of the affirmation and of the productivity, the Act that does not exhaust in any special form, in any particular determination because it returns and perpetually reflects upon itself, and in this reflection it incessantly finds an indefinite virtue of action; in short the Spirit is the affirmative act, free from every matter, the Act in the originality of its autonomy; the Act that, in putting itself, perpetually presupposes itself but nothing else. This is what Fichte means when he affirms that his first principle is contemporarily Subject-Object." [2] Hegel asserts that the Idea is "der Begriff, insofern er sich realisiert." [3] For Hegel "the Idea that is for itself, considered according to this unity with itself, is intuitive. But, as intuition, the Idea is brought into the one-sided determination of immediacy or negation by means of extrinsic reflection. The absolute liberty of the Idea is therefore that it does not pass only into life, nor allow life to appear in it only as a finite knowledge but in the absolute truth of itself it resolves to allow to go freely out of itself, as Nature, the moment of its particularity, or of its determination and of its otherness, the immediate Idea that is its reflection." [4]

Croce repeats neither Kant, nor Fichte, nor Hegel, but he understands the originality of the principle of creativity, abolishes the dualism that one still finds in the German thinkers and maintains the idea of the spirituality of reality.

The view that reality is only spirit is brought out with clearness by Croce with his emphasis on the theory of the predicate of existence. "When being is conceived as something external to the human spirit and knowledge as separable from its object, so that the object could exist without being known, it is evident that the existence of the object becomes a datum, something, as it were, placed before the spirit, something given to the spirit, extraneous to it, and which the spirit could never make its own if it did not, summoning courage and faith, swallow the bitter morsel by an irrational act of faith. And the entire philosophy, as we go on unfolding it, shows that there is nothing outside the spirit, and there are therefore no data confronting it. The same conceptions of the external, mechanical and natural world are not external data but data of the same spirit. The spirit fashions that so-called 'external' world because it enjoys fashioning it, and it re-annuls it when it has no more joy in it." [5]

Croce deepens the idealistic conception of life. In opposition to positivism which frowns upon the idea of the distinction Croce makes it important. He divides the spirit into theoretical and practical activities; the theoretical into intuitive and logical acts; the practical into economic and moral manifestations. "Human knowledge has two forms: it is intuitive or logical knowledge; knowledge through the *fantasia* or knowledge through the intellect; knowledge of the individual or knowledge of the universal; knowledge of the individual things or of their relationships: in short, it is productive of images or productive of concepts. . . . Even the practical activity divides itself into two forms: the first is the purely economic activity; the second is the moral activity. Economics is like the Aesthetics of the practical activity; Morality is like the Logic of the theoretical activity." [6] Croce is very hostile to sociological positivism. The positivists consider sociology as the science of the explanatory principles of history; Croce considers philosophy such a science, and if the positivists look upon sociology as a metaphysics Croce reduces it to a certain discipline of schematic or naturalistic character, and when the positivists are proud of the new term "sociology" Croce states that such a term is barbaric; that the term "political science" would be more palatable. "He was so ruthless in his fight against the shallow generalizations of the positivistic sociology of his youth that sociological studies in Italy have still to recover from the discredit to which he brought them in the common opinion." [7] Croce opposes the positivistic conception of art. The positivists viewed art as a pleasure deriving from psychological associations, a pleasure deriving from habits or hereditary dispositions. There were even those who reduced art to sexuality or prehistoric animality or insanity. For Lombroso great mental efforts produce physiological disorders in the organism, and the disorders are disease, degeneration, folly, and therefore art is identical with disease, degeneration, folly. Croce sees art in a different light. For him art is knowledge of the particular or individual. Croce is adverse to positivistic antihistoricism. Positivism despises history; Croce exalts it as a severe discipline. "The positivists ignored the history of philosophy, treated the great thinkers of the past with barbaric vulgarity as if they were a poor people, pagans who had not received the benefit of the new gospel (the third era of humanity which succeeds the 'mythological' and the 'metaphysical' one), and when by chance they tried to narrate history history was always conventional and imaginary. All this induced me to think that positivism, rather than a reasonable doctrine, was a 'state of the soul,' a mixture of ignorance and pride: a rebellion against the rigor and the severity of historical knowledge." [8] At times Croce does not even feel the necessity of

exalting history: he finds history in the human heart
and mind. Everyone is a historian when he tries to
satisfy a need of his spirit by sympathizing with a certain present or past historical experience: if he is
liberal his heart will palpitate with the heart of
Mazzini; if he is Catholic his heart will be in unison
with that of Saint Thomas. At times Croce also feels
the need to minimize the world of the natural sciences
by contrasting them to the world of philosophy. Croce
affirms that philosophy is cognitive but the natural
sciences are essentially utilitarian. They measure, cal-
culate, fashion classes and types, formulate laws, show
how a fact is derived from another, but they find
themselves helpless before facts which are appre-
hended by thought. If philosophy grasps the essence
of reality, the natural sciences only create useful abstractions. "When the natural sciences seek to constitute themselves perfect sciences, they must leap out
of their circle and pass into philosophy. This they do
when they posit concepts which are not naturalistic,
such as the unextended atom, the aether or vibrating
medium, vital force, imperceptible space, etc. . . .
true and proper philosophic efforts when they are
not meaningless words. The natural concepts are,
without doubt, very useful, but they are incapable of
knowing the essence of the spirit." [9]

In the history of philosophy there is a philosopher
whom Croce recognizes as his precursor: Bergson.
For the French philosopher the scientific concept is
useful or relative, but not cognitive or absolute. In
Bergson "est relative la connaissance symbolique par
concepts préexistants qui va du fixe au movant mais
non pas la connaissance intuitive, qui s'installe dans le
mouvement et adopte la vie même des choses. Cette
intuition atteint l'Absolu." [10] It is clear that in both

philosophers the point of departure is different. In Bergson the idea of the practicality of science is based on the criterion of the intellect as a mediate but not immediate knowledge; in Croce the concept of science as something economic is founded on the distinction of practical and theoretical activity.

Croce and Bergson belong to the economic-scientific school whose representatives are Poincaré, Boutroux, Rickert, Le Roy, Avenarius and Mach. Rickert defines the scientific concept as "a means for a scientific purpose." The world of bodies is infinite in time and space, and it is impossible to represent it in its extensive or intensive essence. The naturalistic concept tries to overcome the infinity by formulating a series of judgments. The naturalistic methodology is also applied to the field of psychology and sociology where the concepts of soul and society replace the wealth and concreteness of human spirituality. To the same conclusion comes Le Roy. For him the rigorous necessity which constitutes the pride of the natural science is not something scientific, but it is decreed: a decree that has the practical purpose of mastering the single facts and of communicating with other men. Avenarius considers science as a simple description of the forms of experience and the intellectual process as an instrument that alters the pure and primitive experience (the pure perception) in order to classify. In Mach physics, zoology and botany have as their unique foundation the description of the natural phenomena, phenomena in which there are never equal cases, and if they are, they are created in the light of the schematic [11] imitation of reality which gives origin to the concept of bodies, things, concepts that are our mental constructions. This economic schematism is the strength but also the weakness of science

because in presenting the facts it sacrifices their individuality and real physiognomy and it only looks for
the exactness required by a determinate case.

We are also tempted to recall some other historical
precedents. Kant, who was well versed in the field of
mathematics and natural sciences, analyzed the
method of the exact sciences and he pointed out their
limits, relegating the problem of immortality to the
practical reason; Jacobi, who studied the greatest
monument of exact science applied to speculative
problems, Spinoza's philosophy, demonstrated that we
cannot come out of the finite, that God and morality
are the object of feeling; Goethe felt the emptiness of
the intellectualistic Enlightenment and spoke of a
completely animated nature; Hegel and Schelling did
not consider the natural sciences as sufficiently scientific, and they held that it is the function of scientific
philosophy to make them more scientific.

And Croce accepted this philosophical heritage
and formulated his own philosophy of science.

III

AESTHETICS

Among all the spiritual manifestations that Croce studied one can safely say that the world of art occupied a special place in Croce's heart. It is true that Croce investigated in depth the nature of philosophy, history and morality, but the problem of art was always his favorite problem.[1]

For Croce art is intuition. Intuition is neither perception, nor sensation, nor association; rather it is expression. "It is believed that everyone can imagine a Raphael Madonna, but Raphael has been Raphael for the mechanical ability of painting it. Nothing is more false." [2] The world which one ordinarily intuits is a small thing. Should one intuit his experiences very deeply, he would express himself very profoundly.

Croce had an idea of art which, viewed in the light of the end of the nineteenth century, was a real discovery. During that time art was confused with naturalism, hedonism, philosophy or morality: this confusion was so strong that it was reflected by writers such as Zola, Verga, Galdós, Fogazzaro, D'Annunzio and others. Croce strongly criticizes these fashionable doctrines. Croce criticizes the naturalistic aesthetics because this aesthetics considers art as a physical thing, a concrete, material object. Preoccupied with art as something objective, these naturalists, for example, hold that certain colors are more aesthetic than others, certain determinate figures are more beautiful than others, certain sounds are more melodious than others. The naturalistic aesthetics tries to naturalize art, when nature, says Croce, does not exist. "Should anyone doubt my statement, I would answer that nature has no existence whatsoever and that art, to which many devote their lives and which fills everyone's heart with joy, is very real; therefore art cannot be a physical thing which is something unreal." [3] Croce criticizes the hedonistic aesthetics, an aesthetics which reduces art to pleasure. By its own nature, says Croce, pleasure is not artistic. Art is neither the pleasure of a good dinner, nor the pleasure of a "walk in the open air which restores warmth to our body and makes the blood circulate faster in our veins, nor is it the practical achievement of a dream in our heart and so forth." [4] Croce criticizes the value of the moralistic aesthetics. Since, says Croce, art is a theoretical and not a practical act, it is concerned only with feeling and not concerned with moral action. Croce says: "Indeed, art, as the ancients already observed, is not born of an act of the will; the good will which constitutes the good man does not constitute the artist." [5] What does constitute a great artist is the natural ability to feel powerfully and profoundly. Morality, being dependent upon the free will, is within everyone's power. But the artist, who must be able to feel deeply, is either born with this ability or he is not. If he lacks it, he can never achieve greatness as an artist. Croce criticizes the intellectualistic aesthetics. The intellectualistic aesthetics, says Croce, reduces art to intellectual knowledge. Intellectual knowledge for Croce is always philosophical, and, as such, realistic. Conceptual knowledge differentiates between possibility and impossibility, between reality and unreality. But art, understood as intuition, "means indistinction of reality and unreality, the image with its color of pure image, the pure ideality of the image." [6]

In the light of Crocian intuition, a profound and original theory, many aesthetic problems receive a new meaning, interpretation or color. In regard to the problem of form and content Croce affirms that there is no difference between the two things. A good content or a deep feeling always expresses itself in good form. Therefore Croce opposes the German *Gehaltsaesthetik* which identifies the content with the logical act or concept, the idea or the speculative concept; contrasts Berenson's distinction between the "illustrative" and the "decorative" element in the realm of painting; rejects the *ars rethorica* because it conceives the literary form as the body of thought or feeling. The classification of the arts is absurd. The important thing is the artist's feeling, whether he creates a tragedy or a comedy, an epic or a statue. "The so-called arts have no aesthetic limits because in order to have them they should also have aesthetic existence, and we have demonstrated the empirical genesis of those partitions. Therefore any attempt of the aesthetic classification of the arts is absurd. If they do not have limits they are not determinable, nor are they philosophically classifiable. All the volumes of classifications and systems of the arts could be (with due respect to the writers who have sweated over this) burned without any harm." [7] Translation is declared an impossibility. Poetry is not water which one can pour from one vase into another. Poetry is individuality, quality, uniqueness. "We can elaborate logically what we first have elaborated only in an aesthetic form, but we cannot reduce what has already had its aesthetic form to another aesthetic form. Every translation either weakens and wastes an expression or creates a new expression putting the first expression in the crucible and mixing it with the other impressions which belong to the translator. In the first case the expression always remains one because the other is more or less deficient, that is, not a true expression; in the second case there will be two expressions but of two different contents." [8] Genius and taste are declared identical. "The difference between genius and taste only consists in the diversity of circumstances: one is a productive activity; the other is a reproductive activity. The activity that judges is called taste; the productive activity is called genius: genius and taste are therefore called identical." [9] The traditional literary criticism is rejected. The critic must approach the poet's world and he must search for the "nota fondamentale," the fundamental motif, and he must not reduce poetry to a complex of historical observations or linguistic minutiae. Also the critic must not show the superiority of a poet's artistic world over that of another. If poetry is the expression of feeling a poetical world cannot be compared with another. "Every individual, that is, every moment of the spiritual life of an individual has its artistic world, and this artistic world cannot be compared with others." [10] It is true that Dante's world is more complex than that of Petrarch, but the world of Dante does not have the mundane quality of that of Petrarch. It is true that Saint Francis of Assisi does not have Ariosto's style, but the same Ariosto is incapable of creating the candid, tender world of the great saint. The natural beauty is destroyed. For Croce beauty is a projection of the human spirit. Things are neither beautiful nor ugly, but the spirit creates both beauty and ugliness. "An artist is enraptured before a beautiful landscape; another before a rag merchant's shop; one before a girl's gracious face; another before the lurid face of an old rascal. The first will say that the rag merchant's shop and the rascal's lurid face are majestic; the second will say that the beautiful landscape and the girl's face are insipid." [11] Language is poetry. Language is not a complex of ideas or concepts or abstractions, but a texture of images, metaphors, and as such, of poetical nature. "Language is essentially poetry and art: with language, with the artistic expression man grasps individual reality, that unique vibration that the spirit intuits and which it does not actualize in terms of concepts, but as sounds, tones, colors, lines and so forth. Therefore language, understood in its true nature and in its whole extension, is adequate to reality. The illusion of inadequacy is born when the language is confused with the fragment of the language, as something separated from the organism to which it belongs. Thus paper, this paper of which I speak is not only the words that 'this paper' express, separated from the rest and abstract, but what my eyes, or better, what my whole spirit sees and which it represents through sounds, colors, etc." [12] A model language is discarded. For Croce language is neither the imitation of nature, nor an external object, but spirituality, and as such, every man speaks according to his own attitudes or back-

ground. "To seek a model language is to seek immobility in movement. Everyone speaks and must speak
in the light of the echoes that things arouse in his
soul, that is, according to his impressions. Without
doubt when the most convinced supporter of whatever solution of the problem of the unity of the
language (the latinized language, the language of the
fourteenth century or the Florentine one) speaks in
order to communicate his thoughts and to make himself understood he feels that, in substituting the language which responds to his own impressions with the
Latin, Florentine word or with the word of the fourteenth century, he will falsify these impressions; he is
not a speaker any longer but a vain listener of himself,
not a serious but a pedantic man, not a sincere man
but a histrionic." [13] The mortality of art is repudiated.
For Croce art is a manifestation of the spirit, and as
such, eternal. Man will create artistically as long as he
lives. "The question of whether art is mortal or immortal has no meaning for us. Once one has admitted
that the artistic function is a necessary aspect of the
spirit the question resembles the other question
whether sensation or intelligence is eliminable or
not." [14]

The concept of pure intuition which really penetrates the essence of art is shaken, endangered, compromised by other contradictory aesthetic theories.
Croce will say that art is cosmos, organicism, universality. "Every pure artistic representation is itself and
the universe, the universe as an individual form, and
the individual form as the universe." [15] Art or artistic
representation is individuality, and as such it cannot
exist outside the cosmos; art is a finite thing, and as
such it cannot exist outside the infinite; art is a voice
and a part of the soul, and as such it cannot exist out-

side the whole. According to the Hegelian and Crocian dialectics, the part does not exist outside the
whole. One cannot "break reality into appearance
and essence, interior and exterior, accident and substance, manifestation and force, finite and infinite,
sensible and suprasensible, matter and spirit and
other terms." [16] In the artistic image palpitates the
life of the universe. In a truly poetical verse one can
find the entire human history, a history made of
sorrow and joy, tears and smiles, illusions and reality.
As a water drop has in itself all the chemical elements
which form the ocean, so an artistic representation
contains in itself all the elements from which is
woven the drama of human existence. Croce will say
that art is morality. "The moral conscience is the
foundation of poetry." [17] The artist must have the
feeling of good and bad, of purity and impurity, of
hell and paradise. Most likely the artist will not be a
hero, but he should feel the beauty of courage; he
will not be a patriot, but he must feel the dignity of
patriotism; he may not be an excellent friend, but
he must feel the beauty of friendship. In short, the
poet cannot close his soul to the moral world because
a world which does not take into account morality is
a chaos where the light of poetry glimmers wanly and
goes out. Without morality a poet will not be "a personality, but a caricature." [18] A world in which there
are not present moral factors is not a human world.
A world in which there is no interplay of the forces
of good and evil, of virtue and vice, of vulgarity and
spirituality is not an artistic world. Only an artist
endowed with a moral sensibility can change an inor-
ganic into an organic world, a chaos into a cosmos.
An artist who does not believe in moral values can
create personages living a confused and undifferen-

tiated life, but not characters whose life is harmonic and creative. All the truly great artists, from Aeschylus to Goethe, believe in the hierarchy of values. The artist cannot create a world which lacks the moral afflatus. Morality resembles a sun ray which shines in the darkness of passion, and passion changes itself into a human ideal. Without moral sensibility the artist will create an artificial artistic life, a life of empty and obtuse intelligence, that is to say, a life which lacks the warmth of humanity. Croce almost comes close to Shelley and Schiller. Shelley considered poetry as the perpetual source of intellectual life; he thought poetry to be a beneficial and necessary divinity in a world which is essentially materialistic; he celebrated the necessary harmony between reason and imagination but he also saw art as the creation of moral values. Schiller was essentially concerned with the problem of nature and freedom, sensibility and morality, necessity and liberty; he was caught between the rationalistic spirit of the French Revolution and the savagery of the masses, but he also looked upon art as an activity which was neither nature, nor morality, but the road to morality. Croce will say that art is "poetic expression." Art moves in the particularity of passion and in the cosmic totality. "Poetry includes particular and universal, embraces sorrow and pleasure, and above the contrasting elements of reality the vision of the whole emerges, above the contrast the harmony, above the narrowness of the finite the land of the infinite." [19] Art is like a bird. The bird sings for the sake of singing but in its singing it expresses its whole being, all its instincts, its whole nature. Likewise the poet is an artist but he is also a man. As a moral man has a logical and artistic capacity, as a philosopher has a poetical life and a moral conscience, so the poet nourishes his soul with thought, morality and the "spirare tragicum." [20] Thought, morality and pathos knock at the door of art. Art or intuition receives and transforms these voices into a world which is deeper and richer as one sees in Homer, Shakespeare, Dante and Goethe. Therefore Croce opposes impressionism, pure poetry and decadentism. Impressionism centers itself on a world strewn with impressions or feelings not fully integrated in the realm of the spirit: an art which satisfies itself with the pathos rather than with the ethos. Pure poetry intends not to poetize in the traditional way, refuses the connection between sound and image, degrades the word to pure sound and denies the necessity of feeling. Decadentism is an aristocratic sickness when poetry, says Croce, is health, life,[21] humanity.[22]

Croce lived a truly aesthetic drama. But if the Crocian aesthetics presented a great conflict, a conflict which, in my opinion, was the result of Croce's search for the autonomy of the spiritual category and for the unity of the spirit, his theory of intuition was also in conflict. Croce will assert that intuition is also the representation of desire. "Desires and emotions, as we know, are of the same stuff and art represents this stuff." [23] Therefore Croce stops to admire Tasso's world. In Tasso's poetry "beyond the fascination of the Armidas there is the aspiration, the nostalgia, the desperate passion for the tall and proud woman, arrogant in her virtue, despising the sentimental feebleness and entirely concerned about civic enterprises: a passion for the woman whom one will never possess either physically or spiritually." [24] Croce resembles Freud. For Freud [25] art is the expression of desires which, like a subterranean river, lie below the surface

of the human rationality. It is clear that while Freud
develops this concept, Croce leaves it at an embryonic
stage.

This is the living struggle of Croce, a burning personal need for finding the essence of art and the
essence of intuition. But another problem remained,
and a very crucial one. How does the artistic process
take place? Does the artist reproduce or create? Is the
artist a receptive or an active entity? Is art a repro-
duction or a creation? It was evident that with the
conception of art-intuition Croce conceived art as
imitation. The artist intuits because he feels deeply.
The fantasy imitates or reproduces a world of impressions. "The expression is always based on the
impressions directly. He who conceives a drama
gathers a great number of impressions: the same
expressions, some other times conceived, are fused
together with the new ones." [26] Croce did not feel
at ease at the presence of this problem and after 1919
he tried to deepen his understanding of the problem
of the origin of art, something only touched upon in
his previous works. Art became creation. "In posing
and resolving problems (imaginative or aesthetic) art
does not imitate something which already exists, but
produces something new, creates a new spiritual situation and therefore is not imitation, but creation." [27]
The poet does not create concepts, abstractions or con-
ventions, however; rather he creates a new spiritual
tone; therefore he is a creator and not an imitator.

IV

LITERARY CRITICISM

Croce lived his aesthetic theories in the unity of his mental and practical life. Similar to De Sanctis who meditated on the aesthetic and artistic problems with seriousness and tenacity, Croce became the living example of the perfect identification between the philosophy of art and artistic analysis. Therefore Croce's diagnosis of literature is not different from the fundamental postulates of his aesthetics.

What is one of the fundamental postulates? Art is intuition. Intuition is the knowledge of the individual or the representation of feeling. Croce is aware of his opposition to French criticism. French literary critics are alert to the impressions of art, to its uniqueness, but they identify art with practical life, the *fantasia* with the psychology of the artist, the history of poetry with that of social feelings, customs or culture. In Virgil, Sainte-Beuve sees the sophisticated Roman; in Homer, the primitive Greek. "Car de même que qu'Omère est le premier de grands viellards et des aveugles harmonieux qui, tenant une lire,

chantent et font leurs recits dans les assemblées
publiques et les festins; que la foule qui les presse et
les écoute inspire, et en qui l'improvisation et la
composition se confondent dans la vivacité et la
présence d'esprit d'une memoire enchanteresse; de
même Virgil est et sera toujours le premier des poëtes
qui composent dans la chambre et le cabinet, qui
étudient longuement et se recueillent, qui corrigent
beaucoup y n'improvisent jamais." [1] Croce reads the
same shortcoming in De Sanctis. De Sanctis views
Italian art as the mirror of Italian moral life. In him
Dante becomes the poet of the austere Italy of the
communes, Franciscan mysticism, Thomistic thought;
Parini is the first Italian of the *Risorgimento*. Croce
opposes the Italian critical school of D'Ovidio, Carducci, Zumbini, Monaci, Ascoli, Bartoli and Rajna.
D'Ovidio, says Croce, does not look for the individual
physiognomy of an artistic work but he loses himself
in academic questions. "Instead of asking himself
whether the art of Manzoni is as profound as that of
Shakespeare or as harmonious as that of Virgil or
Ariosto D'Ovidio poses these questions: 'Is there any
Walter Scott, Cervantes or Carlo Potta influence in
Manzoni? What part did Manzoni play in active
politics? What are his intentions in creating the figure
of Brother Galdino?' " [2] Croce contrasts the German
critical school. With their philosophical preparation
the German critics (W. Scherer, Hettner, Julian
Schmidt) searched for the essence of a work of art, but
they often forgot the form for the content, replaced
the history of poetry with that of philosophy and lost
the individual quality of the artistic work. The
German critics were under the influence of Hegel.
"We must maintain that it is art's function to reveal
truth under the mode of art's sensuous or material

configuration, to display the reconciled antithesis previously described, and by this means to prove that it possesses its final aim in itself, in this representation in short and self-revelation." [3]

One can state that guided by the concept of intuition, which has a solid foundation in the realm of the impressions, Croce examines the art of Matilde Serao. "In her youth and adolescence Matilde Serao has observed the families of the Neapolitan petite bourgeoisie, the shopkeepers, the thin employees, the poor lawyers, the poor professors, the pensionaries, the decent poverty that finds a hard time in making ends meet." [4] For Croce Serao receives these Neapolitan experiences and elaborates them with her *fantasia*. In his view, Serao gathers these sensations and enlivens them with her heart: a heart that is full of tenderness and compassion for the sufferings and trepidations of those who live in a world of constant sacrifice.

For Croce, does Serao's art consist in the representation of impressions? Croce is very careful about identifying art with our daily experiences, a solution that one finds among modern impressionists, but at the same time he is very conscious of the fact that without the impressions, *la vita vissuta*, art would have no matter to work on. For Croce, Serao's art is born because the matter becomes the form, the sensation the expression, the impression the intuition.

In a similar way Croce looks at Fucini's art. Fucini narrates his youthful experiences. When he was a university student he gambled the tuition money given to him by his poor father, who was a doctor in a small mountain town. He returns home in order to ask for more money. The following morning, a dark and snowy wintry morning, he is awakened and told

that his father is waiting for him outside. "I ran
toward the door and, in the light of the lantern with
which the servant illuminated the night, there before
me I saw my father on the horse, immobile, wrapped
in his big mantle covered with snow:—Take,—he said
to me, talking and making a furrow in my soul at
every word.—Take . . . now it is your money . . .
But before spending it . . . look at me!—and he ful-
minated me with a fiery and melancholic look. Before
spending the money remember how your father earns
it." [5] Croce sees this as intense feelings transformed
into images.

The concept of *fantasia* or intuition is followed
by Croce's theory of art as cosmos. Here we must
make a reservation of a speculative character. The
term "cosmos" now means the universe in its materiality, now it means the artist's life perspective.
Croce seems to have been entangled in this confusion
during his whole life. But here we will sidestep this
confusion and accept Croce's thought in its substance.
He always considered the spirit as the unique reality,
and therefore, the term "cosmos" must be interpreted
in the sense of one's mental outlook, thought, world-
view. This can be seen in Croce's analysis of Goethe.

For Croce the greatness of Goethe's artistic world
does not consist in the interest in a particular realm
of feelings, a special credo, a certain historical situation but in the supreme interest in the dynamic
rhythm of things, the eternal motion of the universe,
the energetic spectacle of the world, a spectacle that
Goethe does not observe with Ariosto's detachment,
but with his *strebende Seele,* with his constant will to
ascend perpetually and with his love for the future in
preference to the past. "This grandiose moral and
mental ascension, beyond and above poetry, confers on

Goethe the impress that makes him distinct and unique with regard to other poets of his class. In Goethe life and thought completely dissolve themselves in poetry, and if something remains outside, this has little importance, because it is a highly personal thing or feelings or concepts common to the times." [6]

The firm consciousness of the cosmic character of art, an art that is more complex than the intuitive one, gave Croce the opportunity to free himself, almost with a gesture of dismissal, of everything that was not great poetry. Therefore one can understand why Croce spoke of Cervantes and Goethe as the "great voices of the centuries," and if later he examined the poets and writers of the "periodo umbertino" one notices more nostalgia for the past than a real enthusiasm for their work. It is natural that once one has seen the mountain tops he is not too fervent in gazing at the hills.

But a great part of Croce's literary criticism is spent in closing the gap between intuitive and cosmic art, and instead of eliminating one of the two, he still offers us an art that is cosmic and intuitive. Croce was a profound thinker but in this case he holds a theory that maintains two opposite views.

Croce's books on Ariosto and Dante are a sufficient example to demonstrate this contradiction. On one hand Dante is supreme when he represents Francesca's love, a love which is not made of straw, but a love which is reality and imagination, joy and torment, a love which is neither bestiality, nor divinity, but rather humanity. Dante touches the heights of great poetry when he represents Farinata's heroism. Farinata is the "defender of his faction, of his political ideal." [7] Florence still burns his soul, and he cares neither for Cavalcante's sorrow, nor for the infernal terror. His heart is shut off from every other feeling. However, when Dante loses himself in syllogisms, he is a philosopher, but not a poet. On the other hand Dante's art is a cosmic art: an art that yearns for the eternal and the infinite. On one hand, Ariosto is a true poet not when he celebrates the d'Este family, but when he sings of harmony, a harmony which is not a love of concepts, but sensible harmony. In Ariosto the sensible harmony is identified with love for a beautiful corporeal form, for smiling eyes and a gracious face; in Ariosto harmony is a feeling among feelings, and it constitutes the core of his soul. Ariosto shows the soul of a poet not when he cries over the misfortunes of his native land, not when he complains of the Church, but when he sings the world of beauty. "If Ariosto had been a philosopher, he would have celebrated Harmony, a celebration unequalled in the history of literature, singing that high Idea which made him understand the discordant harmony of things, and, satisfying his mind, gave peace and joy to his spirit." [8] On the other hand, Ariosto is the poet in whom "Harmony operated to reduce the delightful chivalrous stories and the capricious tricks to poetry, the small narrative or erotic poetry to a more complex poetry, and to mediate the immediate, transforming those different classes of particular feelings." [9]

If in the problem of art as cosmos Croce was confused and contradictory, he is more secure in establishing his other theory of art as morality. He is very decisive in stating that Tasso's art is great because it has an ethical or religious quality.[10] Croce also notices that the same struggle between voluptuousness and glory,[11] pleasure and duty, enjoyments and austere virtue is not something superficial, but is very artistic.

Croce is assertive in condemning the art of the seventeenth century. An art, says Croce, that has no religious or ethical ideals, that is not aware of the contrasts that nourish these ideals, cannot be a real art. And the same Croce adds that Metastasio was a superficial but not a real artist. Metastasio's Zenobia, who, forced to choose between the life of her husband and that of her lover, prefers the first one, but does not want to hear the name of the other whom she abandons to death, lacks moral substance.

This concept of art as morality was not to be Croce's last aesthetic theory. There was a fourth aesthetics to come. For if art is morality, by what right does one want to eliminate thought and pathos? Could Shakespeare without them have portrayed Hamlet's drama? Can an artist represent a world where pathos and thought are not an integral part? Aware of this difficulty Croce began to speak of art as "poetic expression": an art that is intuition and ethos, thought and pathos.

Croce felt this theory very deeply. He saw it everywhere: in Cervantes, Virgil, Lucretius and Homer. "Homer's heroes know that sooner or later they must dry their tears and take again their part in life because destiny made man's heart to suffer. . . . Homer also knows an ultraworld included in the same world, and this is the fame, the glory, the song of the poets, the name on the lips of men and women, the remembrance in the heart . . . the Iliad is 'poetry,' untamed poetry; the Odyssey is 'literature,' tamed poetry." [12] To Croce Lucretius appears as the poet in whom the philosophical and historical investigations mingle with the passionate element, as the poet in whom the preparation, the development and the conclusion of research mixes with a passion that is now effusive, now reserved. Besides thought there is a sincere impetus of redemption, sorrow and a feeling of devotion toward the *"tu pater, es rerum inventor, tu patria nobis,"* toward the benefactor of humanity.

This aesthetics is richer than the theory of art as morality. This theory of art as morality seems to be a sterile land, and one is tempted to put it aside. It takes more than moral sensibility in order to create a work of art. We do not imply that this aesthetics has no meaning in Croce's intellectual life. Everything has a meaning, and therefore even this theory has a significance in Croce's spiritual world. The theory of art as morality prepared him to elaborate his concept of art as "poetic expression."

V

LOGIC

Still, as Croce grew older and more sure of himself, he felt, of course, the need to investigate the problem of the pure concept. To Croce aesthetics was fascinating, but at the bottom of his soul he felt that the problem of logic was also very important. And his genius was called into action by his great awareness of this problem.

For Croce the pure concept is concept, universality and concreteness. Concept is neither feeling nor intuition. This differentiates the pure concept from any immediate knowledge or any alogical experience: the concept is thought. Universality is neither generalization nor empiricism. This differentiates the concept from natural sciences. Concreteness is neither fiction nor abstraction, but reality itself. This diferentiates the pure concept from the mathematical sciences. "The concept is concept, that is, is not feeling, enrapture or intuition or any other similar spiritual alogical state, a state which is deprived of demonstrative force . . . the concept is universal and not merely general: it must not be confused with the general representations such as 'house,' 'horse,' 'blue,' things which are barbarically called concepts . . . the concept is concrete: it is not the skeleton of reality, but the comprehension of it in its full fullness and richness." [1]

And one must notice that the series of mathematical and scientific concepts is criticized. In criticizing them Croce determines their character with great clarity.

The scientific concepts—cat, dog—each represent a group of objects, but although the characteristics in each group may be innumerable and their varieties indeterminable there is nothing indicated by their common name which reveals a nature over and above the representative character of each of the objects. The purpose of these concepts is to help us to classify objects or animals, and the means by which the term is made to serve this purpose is either the choice of some particular representation as representative of all the others or the formation of a generalization of all the different things or animals that we class together. In either case the concept is concrete but not universal. The mathematical concepts—geometrical triangle, free movement—are the contrary. They do not denote a group of representations nor a single representation. There is no representative element in them at all, that is to say, no single representation and no possible group of representations could exhaust them. "It seems that with them we leave behind the embarrassments of sense representations. The triangle and free movement are not things of which we can state the characteristics and to which we can set definite limits and which have a beginning and an end in time. As far as thought can go, whenever reality is thinkable, the concepts of triangle and free movement have validity. The triangle takes place whenever three straight lines intersect to include a space and form three angles, the sum of which, though one triangle may vary from another, is equal to the sum of two right angles. It is impossible to confuse the triangle with the square or the circle. Free movement is a movement thought of as taking place without obstacle of any kind. It is impossible to confuse it with a movement to which there is any kind of obstacle." [2] These mathematical concepts have universality but they lack concreteness. There is no such thing as a geometrical triangle in reality, because in reality there are no straight lines, no rectangles and sums of rectangles and sums of angles equal to two rectangles. A free movement does not exist in reality because every free movement is determined by certain conditions or obstacles.

The difference between the pure concept and the pseudo-concept, a term that Croce coins for the natural-mathematical concept, is not that the one is true and the other is false, but that the one is a form of knowledge and the other is not. While in Hegel the pseudo-concept is an abstraction but still an inferior thought, in Croce it has only a practical value.

For Croce the pure concept is distinction. Croce is aware of the contributions of Vico, Schelling and Herbart. Vico divides the spirit, language, government into a series of distinct concepts: the spirit is sense, imagination, mind; language is divine, heroic, articulate; government is theocratic, aristocratic, democratic. Schelling divides reality into a series of powers or degrees. In virtue of its nature the subject-object objectifies, but it conquers every objectivity and more and more acquires a more powerful subjectivity until, after exhausting every potentiality, appears as a triumphant subject. Herbart became aware that the Fichtian *Ichheit* was inert, empty and incapable of creating the contrast which creates the spiritual life. To the *Ichheit* he opposed the necessary moment of the serious distinction. To the question in what does the theory of the distinct concepts differ from the theory of the opposites, Croce answers very clearly. In the theory of the distinct concepts the concept a can stay without the concept b, but the concept b cannot stay without the concept a. Let us take two concepts that Croce studied all his life: the concept of art (poetry, language, intuition) and the concept of philosophy (prose, logic, thought). For Croce poetry can stay without prose, but prose cannot stay without poetry; art can stay without philosophy, but philosophy cannot stay without art. Every philosophy, says Croce, does not exist except on words, images, metaphors, that is, language. If we now pass, continues Croce, from the theory of the distinct concepts a and b to the synthesis of the opposites A, B, C (being, non-being, becoming) we can see the difference between the two theories. The concept a can stay without b, but b cannot stay without a. Instead, A and B, outside of C, cannot exist, that is, they are not two concepts, but two abstractions: the only real concept is C. In the first case we have a dyad; in the second case we have a triad; in the first case we have two real concepts; in the second case we have two abstractions and one real concept.

The pure concept is also opposition. The only truth is that thought or reality has no opposition before it, but it has opposition in itself; that without opposition reality is not reality. "Unity is the positive, opposition is the negative, but the negative is also positive, positive insofar as negative, and were it not true, one would not understand the fullness of the positive." [3] Without error there is no truth; without sorrow there is no real happiness; without ugliness there is no concrete beauty. Croce is conscious of his debt to previous philosophers. Böhme asserted the idea of opposition with great vigor. "But the fundamental opposition whose union takes place in the Divinity is the moral-religious opposition between Good and Evil. This opposition pervades the whole universe and there is 'nothing in nature which does not contain Good and Evil.' Böhme's favorite example is that of the fire whose good and pleasing aspect is not in harmony with the ferocious and ruinous heat, and if on the one hand it is the element of life, on the other hand it is the element of destruction. If therefore all things have in themselves the opposition of the fundamental qualities of Good and Evil it is necessary to conclude that this opposition must have already been contained in God who constitutes the intimate essence of things, and it is the vital lymph of the whole tree of the universe." [4] Hamann showed a great dissatisfaction with the principle of identity. Bruno stressed the idea of the *coincidentia oppositorum*. "We do not enjoy ourselves with a specific color but with one that includes all the colors. We do not enjoy ourselves with a specific voice but with a complex voice which is the result of the harmony of other voices. We do not enjoy ourselves with a specific knowable but with one that includes all the knowables, with an apprehensible that includes all the apprehensibles." [5] Hegel saw in opposition the essence of reality. "In the light of his logical doctrine that transforms the theory of opposites into the conception of reality as development Hegel cannot con-

sider the negative term, the aspect of the non-being as
something that faces or as something separated from
the concept of being. If the negative term did not
exist, there would be no development, and reality,
and with it the positive term, would fall. The negative term is the source of development: the opposition
is the same soul of reality." [6] Thus in Croce the pure
concept or thought becomes distinction-opposition,
affirmation-negation, identity-contradiction.

Let us return to Croce's main theme: thought is
synthesis *a priori*. Synthesis *a priori* consists of two
elements: analytical and synthetical judgment, idea
and fact, the truth of reason and the truth of fact,
the concept and the representation, or to use Croce's
expression, universality and concreteness. Croce was
under Kant's influence, but this influence did not last
for very long. Croce was beginning to have doubts
about the relationship between matter and thought
which were to plague him for several years. If he felt
tortured by this problem, he learned from Gentile
that this was not his problem alone. Gentile had ex-
perienced the same intellectual crisis a few years before. Under Gentile's driving influence Croce tried to
overcome Kant's dualism of matter and spirit, concept
and representation, and in 1909 he began to speak
of the *giudizio individuale,* individual judgment, that
is, the concept as the representation and the representation as the concept. "The logical act is something
spoken, represented, individualized, but when one
divides it into concept and individual judgment not
from an empirical point of view, but from the philosophical one creates two monsters: an unindividual-
ized concept, and therefore inexistent in a concrete
way, and an individual judgment not thought, and
therefore inexistent as an individual judgment." [7]

Therefore the dualism between subject and object, subject and predicate, the real and the ideal, history and philosophy disappears.

Let us take as an illustration one of the concepts already mentioned, the concept of history-philosophy, and ask what Croce means by saying that both history and philosophy are identical. For Croce there is no history without philosophy. How can a historian narrate a historical event without the use of concepts? How can a historian narrate without making use of thought? But philosophy is also history. Without the geographical discoveries, the capitalistic society, the religious wars or the thought of Hume there would be no Kant philosophy. Whether the philosopher likes this or not, he cannot jump out of the historical conditions in which he lives nor can he make not happen the things that have already happened. "These events are in his bones, in his flesh and blood, and he must take account of them, that is, he must know them historically, and the breadth of his philosophy is in proportion to the breadth of his historical knowledge. Should the philosopher not know them or should he only have them in him as facts of life he would be like an animal, that is, the animal that is conditioned by the whole of nature and history, but he does not know it." [8]

But to analyze completely all the implications in Croce's individual judgment would require a special study of Croce's logic, which does not fall within the purpose of this book. If we now return to Croce's general problem of logic and strive to find the real force which moves him in the world of logic it is easy to come to this definite conclusion: Croce was now fighting against the sociological and formalistic logic; now he was attempting to reform the logic of Hegel.

For Lévy-Bruhl the mentality of the savages is not our mentality in its early stage: it is a mentality which follows a different route. While our mentality is rational, the mentality of the savages is collective: a mentality where the power of reflection is completely obscured by the subjection to the power of the collective representations. While our mentality is dualistic, the primitive mentality is mystic: the savage feels himself surrounded by the continuous presence of evil spirits.[9] While our mentality obeys the principle of contradiction, the primitive mentality is indifferent to it. Against Lévy-Bruhl's logical relativism Croce holds the universality of human thought. For Croce man's mind is the same under every sky. The three fundamental forms of formalistic logic are the concept, the judgment and the syllogism. The concept is *identical, anonymous, synonymous, distinct, contradictory,* etc.; the judgment is *individual, particular,* and *universal;* the syllogism has four figures, etc. The concept is an idea, as distinguished from a perception; the judgment is the synthesis of the subject and predicate; the syllogism is the synthesis of the judgments. In this formalistic logic Croce sees nothing but verbalism or grammar. For Croce the true judgment is not the combination of the subject and of the predicate, but is the individual "judgment where the universal penetrates the individual." [10] The judgment "the *Divine Comedy* is a work of art" does not express a grammatical relationship; it expresses the perfect identity between the individual and the universal. Outside the category of art there is no real artistic work. Hegelian logic emphasizes the principle of contradiction. Hegel does not answer the question of how the opposition or contradiction originates. To this question Croce answers with the principle of distinction: opposition originates because the spirit is distinction: the spirit is art, philosophy, economics and morality.

But if Croce's logic is to be seen in its true light one should not neglect his opposition to positivism. The positivists were always talking about science, now using Stuart Mill's inductive method, now Spencer's idea of evolution, now Lombroso's psychology, now Marx's scientific socialism. Under this kind of scientific discipline the ordinary intellectual was expected to become a better man. Actually under this harmful positivistic atmosphere the ordinary intellectual filled his mind with scientific knowledge: a knowledge which had very little meaning. The result was that he became very sterile, and without doing anything, he thought that he could solve the problem of the universe with the scientific concept. It was the time when Spencer's disciples were talking of the passage from *homogeneity* to *heterogeneity*. "Evolution is an integration of matter and a concomitant dissipation of motion; during which the matter passes from an indefinite, incoherent homogeneity to a definite and coherent heterogeneity." [11] Therefore there was arrogance in the cultural life, but also the incapacity to understand the real meaning of some profound problems. The same Croce lived in this atmosphere for almost twenty years and he himself became an enthusiast of the Marxist materialism: a materialism that he later rejected with violence. It was the time of his youth, the time during which one constantly searches for his true attitudes and, sooner or later, he is bound to make a few mistakes. The thing to be taught was not the world of the pseudo-concepts, but the world of the pure concept, not science, but history. "When one clearly understands the diversity between the judgment that is history and the formula that is technique he will see the contrast between humanistic education and scientific-naturalistic education, between a classical school and a technical school in its whole depth and seriousness. The humanistic education is directed toward the formation of man as man, and therefore it plans to teach man the book of life, of life in its continuous movement and enrichment which is history; it plans to put man in harmony with the principle of life, with the creative spirit that is in us. To know the truth is a religious act that one performs with reverence, and to deny or to ignore this act that thinks the universal in the individual, the eternal in the transient, is to ignore or to deny the divine in man, therefore justly the ideal of a knowledge that is only technical is considered materialistic." [12]

VI

HISTORIOGRAPHY

In the first place, in an age of positivism, Croce held firm to what he considered to be the essence of history. "History does not search for concepts, nor does it create concepts; it does not deduce, nor does it induce, but it directs itself *ad narrandum,* but not *ad demonstrandum;* it does not create universals and abstractions, but pure intuitions. The *hic et nunc* and the *individuum omnimode determinatum* is the realm of both art and history. Therefore history is reduced to the universal concept of art." [1] Science demonstrates; history narrates; science universalizes; history individualizes. As Croce felt the impelling necessity to fight the domination of the pseudo-scientific philosophy of Spencer which would hardly recognize any other form of knowledge which was not scientific knowledge he identified the individuality of history with that of art. History represents Napoleon and Caesar, the Renaissance and Alexander, the French Revolution and the Italian Unification: facts which have an individual physiognomy. Croce draws on Vico. For Vico the first poets were historians. "In tal guisa i primi poeti si finsero la favola divina, la più grande di quante mai se ne finsero appresso, cioè Giove, re e padre degli uomini e degli dei, ed in atto di fulminante; sí popolare, perturbante e insegnativa, ch'essi stessi, chel sel finsero, sel credettero e con ispantose religioni, le quali appresso si mostreranno, il temettero, il riverirono e l'osservarono." [2]

Croce constantly stresses the individuality which characterizes history, now against the positivists, now against the disciples of Ranke. To the positivist who always interrogates history in order to know whether a reform is good or bad Croce answers that he is mistaken. One cannot, says Croce, interrogate history in order to satisfy his actual needs: what failed in the past does not necessarily fail in the present; what succeeded in the past does not necessarily succeed in the present. It is impossible, continues Croce, to uproot a fact with its roots in a certain time and place in order to solve present problems. And Croce, in condemning Ranke, holds that history is essentially individuality.

With the passing of a few years Croce begins to speak of another theory: history as philosophy. This took place in the year 1909. History becomes the concrete-universal, the individual-universal, thought. Croce expresses this idea in many different ways. Croce will say that the historian must not be impartial. The historian must be impartial if by it one means the lack of passionateness, but if by impartiality one means the lack of a "world-view" there is no impartiality. History includes the subjective element, and this subjectivity is true impartiality. In the world of history the subjective element is not an evil or a necessary evil as one thinks but is a fundamental

element and to doubt this principle is to show a great
distrust toward thought. "History must always judge
rigorously and must always be subjective energetically
rather than to think about the difficulties and risks
that thought encounters because thought always over-
comes its own difficulties and dangers." [3] Beard [4] also
espouses the same view. "The selection and arrange-
ment of facts—a combined and complex intellectual
operation—is an act of choice, conviction, and interpretation respecting values, is an act of thought." [5]
Croce will say that history is not negativity, but rationality. As the literary critic is only concerned with
beauty, so the historian must not judge negatively,
but positively. His affirmation of the positive fact is
sufficient judgment, and it becomes an indirect moral
judgment whenever the consciousness of the historian
is a moral consciousness without any necessity to
blame or to praise on the object of history. "Historical
consideration, therefore, recognizes of equal right the
Church of the Catacombs and that of Gregory VII,
the tribunes of the Roman people and the feudal
barons, the Lombard League and the Emperor Bar-
barossa." [6] Croce will say that the historian must view
history as progress: a progress which realizes two conditions: the achievement of truth and goodness at
every instant and the continuous doubt about what
has been achieved; the achievement of a perpetual
solution and of a perpetual rebirth of the same problem. "One must avoid the two opposite unilateralities
of an achieved and of an unachieved goal, of the
progressus ad finitum and of the *progressus ad infini-
tum*." [7] The most evident proof of this concept, says
Croce, is given by the world of art and poetry: a
world which is never self-satisfied and which creates
new forms, but nevertheless the created works are

always like goddesses on the serene Olympus, shining with strength and beauty. In every aspect of life the historian who is conscious of the forces of the future looks upon the past with the eyes of the artist: human works are always imperfect and perfect, transient and eternal at the same time. Croce will say that the historian must have empathy. The historian will not understand the history of other men and of other times if he does not relive the needs of those men and times. Likewise future generations will not understand our history if they do not sympathize with us. "The practical need that is at the basis of every historical judgment gives history the character of 'contemporary history,' because though the facts are remote or very remote, history always refers to the need and to the present situation in which those facts propagate their vibrations." [8] If in the historian the feeling of Christian charity, the beauty of honor or the love for democracy is dormant, he will not succeed in representing the true spirit of the Gospels or the French Revolution.

And finally it is necessary to make an important consideration. In the year 1925 Croce begins to feel a little uneasy with a historiography that is only thought. Is not the spirit or thought also politics and morality? Is it possible to divide the spirit into pieces? Conscious of this problem Croce begins to speak of history as an "ethical-political" discipline. We will clarify it. For Croce when a people has faith in a certain ideal there is historical splendor; when a people has no enthusiasm in any specific human endeavor there is decadence. Thus history is not only the history of the State but also the history of religious, moral institutions, myths, legends, feelings and other things. Besides the tradition of Voltaire and

Möser, Croce looks most to Goethe for inspiration. In Goethe he reads that "the proper, unique and profound theme of the history of the world, the theme to which all the other themes are subordinated, consists of the conflict between belief and disbelief. All the epochs in which faith rules are splendid, heartening and fecund for contemporary and future generations; on the other hand all the epochs in which disbelief obtains a poor victory, though for a moment they boast of an apparent splendor, disappear from the remembrance of future generations because no one willingly tortures himself with the knowledge of what is sterile." [9] Both Goethe and Croce believe that religious impetus or enthusiasm which characterizes the great historical epochs is nothing but actual faith in universal ethics, the love of ideal operoseness or, to put it more specifically, the enthusiasm for a mental system.

Among Croce's last two concepts of history there is a fundamental motif which constitutes one of the focal points of his philosophy: the rationality of reality. This motif makes its strength and weight felt against Dilthey, Sorel, Tilgher [10] and Pareto.[11] For these thinkers a culture is intimately connected with general representations, emotional and intellectual constructions more felt than reasoned and deeply rooted in a people's soul: general representations, "world-views," *Weltanschauungen* that, though they embody themselves in the form of political, religious and economic institutions, still preserve their irrational origins. Neither does Croce abandon his fight against Spengler. Spengler thought that he had discovered the true substance, the true historical object of culture. "Culture" is a certain organic way of feeling and thinking, and this organic way is the real

force of history. "Culture" has a life independent of
the people who breathe and live it. "Culture" is a
plant, and, as such, its future course is predetermined.
In Croce, instead, culture is not something separated
from a people's life but it is the people; culture is not
fatalism, but freedom; culture is not a biological organism but it is spirituality or rationality. At times
Croce's hostility assumes a very angry tone. "Another
problem is suffered now by a world that is going
toward animality, toward the brute animality, toward
the brute vitality that wants to vanquish and to sub-
stitute the spirit (the 'spirit' that is the enemy of the
'soul' or life according to the theory and the program
of a modern German philosopher), but the spirit
anxiously struggles in descending into the abyss because the conscience continues to admonish the spirit
to abandon the badly idolized, the impulsively
adopted, the artificially cultivated animal habits and
to restore in itself the simple faith in culture and
humanity."[12]

But if these two conceptions of history were profound, Croce was also a deep interpreter of human
events. Profound is his interpretation of the history
of the kingdom of Naples. In his *Storia del regno di
Napoli* Croce discards the old interpretations of the
old historians: interpretations which have no value
for contemporary man because they reflect interests
which are no longer felt. He also discards the positivistic interpretation of the "Southern problem": an
interpretation which explains the history of the kingdom in the light of the poverty of the land. Croce, in
contrast, shows how, through the Spanish domination
and the suppression of the Neapolitan baronage, a
new political class arises in the Neapolitan realm: a
class which was humanistic in its world outlook,

which had a great public spirit, which rebelled against
the Spanish Inquisition, which educated itself more
and more through Descartes' rationalism and which
honored itself with the names of Pietro Giannone,
Paolo Mattia Doria, Antonio Genovesi and others: a
political class which after the experiment of the Re-
public gave up its love for the Neapolitan autonomy
and embraced the Italian national movement. Profound is his interpretation of the baroque age in
Italy. For him Italians at the time had neither patriotism, nor religious fervor, nor real thought, nor real
literature: even the style in art became abstruse, in-
sincere, baroque. Italians, according to Croce's mind,
lacked moral enthusiasm. Even Florence, which had
been the center of the great moral, intellectual and
artistic life of the Italian Renaissance, satisfied itself
with empty political, social and literary forms. Croce
also centers his attention on foreign countries.
France, Holland and Geneva had a great economic,
political and religious movement. These nations gave
birth to Calvinism, Jansenism, rationalism and international law. On the other hand, Italy had no dream
of political unification, nor aspiration for human dignity and liberty, nor commercial or colonial spirit and
while England, France and Holland had Mazarin,
Cromwell, De Witt, Grotius, Milton, Arnauld, Pascal,
Descartes and Spinoza, Italy did not have any great
mind. "Italy had become a conservative country, that
is, it was living on the ideals and forces of the past:
ideas and forces which did not possess vitality because
vitality is actuality of development and transforma-
tion, and the Italian States, instead, had come to a
standstill: a position that they could not even defend
or maintain." [13] Among Croce's lines there is a pessimistic tone, but not absolutely pessimistic. For Croce

the baroque age was a period of decadence but it was
not lived in vain. If we still feel a great aversion
toward pomposity, exaggeration and complexity, if we
are ready to differentiate between what is baroque and
what is genuine, this is the product of the baroque
historical experience. Profound is Croce's interpretation of the history of nineteenth century Europe once
we neglect his metaphysical idealism. For him during
the last century in Italy and Europe the development
of the human spirit achieved a great momentum: the
ideal of liberty was strong and it was looked upon as
the supreme rule, the supreme guidance and the
supreme criterion of every human endeavor. The
Christian ideal of moral liberty, love and brother-
hood which had been almost intuited by the austere
Stoics, which during the Renaissance had assumed a
mundane color and which during the Enlightenment
had been denied in the light of abstract reason, but
was still working in the concept of fraternity, equality
and liberty, found its full expression in the liberal
movement. The close relationship between these two
"religions" was felt by both the liberals and the liberal
Catholics or despised by the materialists, the racists
and the dictators.

Croce abhorred materialists and dictators as much
as he loved freedom, and his analysis of the entire history of Europe is written in conformity with this
criterion. And he stressed the great virtues of the
liberal Cavour, the sublime enthusiasm of the figure
of Mazzini, and he pointed out the abyss between
the Italian and the German *Risorgimento* and between Cavour and Bismarck. Because of these loves
and abhorrences Croce's *Storia d'Europa* is not only
a historical but also an artistic work, and his art does
not endanger his historical judgment. One also no-

tices Croce's optimism. In his youth he had been be-
wildered, sorrowful, desperate, but in this work as in
many others Croce embraces the world with love and
courage, aware of the beauty and sacredness of life.

Also profound is Croce's interpretation of the history of late nineteenth century Italy. In opposition to
Fascism which called liberal Italy "Italietta," the in-
significant Italy, Croce showed that the ideals of liberal Italy were the same ideals of the men of the
Italian *Risorgimento*. In Croce's pages one also observes his contempt toward all political figures of
illiberal leanings, and since the Fascists loved to portray Crispi as the forerunner of their imperialistic
policy Croce represents the Italian statesman as a
visionary. "Even his love for pomp which was in contrast to the very modest clothes of the previous Italian
cabinet members, his idea of a new Palace of the
Parliament with a solemn hall in whose center a
throne of bronze and gold would be erected as the
symbol of the sublimity and stability of the monarchy
and other things corresponded to his feeling of
grandeur. Someone, shocked at this showy outward
display of fantasy, words and gestures, shook his head,
and, thoughtful and suspecting something pathologi-
cal, pronounced the word: 'megalomania.' " [4]

Croce lived surrounded by his friends and books,
but he suffered from living under Mussolini's regime
and he spoke out against a dictatorship that forced
him to choose a life that was not the product of his
own free determination. In his strong blood fervent
was the need of expansion, of participating in the
social and political life of Italy, of suffering and re-
joicing with his own people, and when he found himself before a liberal or illiberal figure his heart burst
with joy or indignation.

Croce's fresh approach to the problem of the Renaissance and his evaluation of Marxism are also worth mentioning. To those who consider the Renaissance as a Latin movement and the Reformation as a German event, to those who speak of the Italian exteriority and of the German *Innigkeit* that other peoples do not possess, Croce answers that they lower an ideal relationship to a material one, a concept to a contingent fact. Though the Renaissance and the Reformation were essentially the products of the Italians and the Germans, both movements expressed the universal needs of the human spirit. "The drama takes place in the heart of everyone: now man celebrates the mundane and earthly life, the unique reality, the unique beauty; now this same life loses its color before a supernatural world; now man securely enjoys his own strength; now he perceives the nullity of this security." [15] For Croce, Marx altered the concepts of bourgeoisie and proletariat. For Marx the bourgeoisie was bad; the proletariat was good. Croce, instead, demonstrates that the bourgeoisie has a juridical, economic and social meaning, but it has also a moral one: the free competition against the mercantile and protective systems, the mobility of wealth against the immobility of the primogenitures, the technique against the old habits, the desire for comfort that destroys the old castles and enlarges the cities and the democratic feeling that measures man in the light of his intelligence and will. For Croce, Marx crystallized the social classes; rather he transformed them into dialectical and even metaphysical categories. On the other hand, Croce shows that history is not created by classes but by individuals. Humanity creates, develops and renews culture through philosophical fervor, artistic creation, heroic actions and technical inventions. "The masses and the classes are abstractions and they are incapable of thinking and operating, actions which can only be performed by the human concreteness, that is by individuals, and curiously enough, the classes and the masses borrow the thoughts and the wills from the demagogues who are men of flesh and blood and, as such, superior to the masses and classes." [16]

Croce achieved important results in the analysis of Italian and European history. His portrayals of Giolitti, Napoleon III, Kant, Hegel and De Sanctis are as original as they are full of truth. "Kant was oriented toward the physical sciences as the true and proper realm of human knowledge. But he neglected and ignored the history of humanity, and he even had insufficient notions about the history of philosophy itself. He was scarcely sensible to poetry: his poets were Horace and Pope, and he had no experience of the other arts except music which he judged an 'indiscreet art' because it makes itself heard when it is not wanted. By a miracle of critical acuteness, and taking advantage of the new writers on the problem of taste, he pointed out in a negative but in a profound way some characteristics of beauty, but he did not identify it with art, and he conceived art as a play between imagination and intelligence." [17] And truly if someone should make a serious study of the Hegelian movement he would be surprised to find how profound is Croce's interpretation of this German philosopher: "Hegel is the great enemy of those who are not satisfied with life, the sensitive souls, the eternal charlatans and agitators in the name of reason and virtue, and historically speaking, Hegel is the enemy of *Faustism* that proclaims the theory to be gray and the tree of life to be green and that despises truth and science, and instead of being possessed by the heavenly spirit, it falls into the hands of the terrestrial one." [18] On the other hand, it is rather superficial to accuse Croce of making certain mistakes—he does not give importance to music, to the environmental factor—: mistakes that are human. No great historian could pass the test of perfection.

VII

ECONOMICS

As Croce considers aesthetics as the first form of theoretical activity, so he maintains that economics or "volition of the particular" is the first manifestation of practical activity.

In Croce the term "particular" has a specific meaning. By the term "particular" Croce means utility or passion. "The economic will is to want an individual purpose . . . an example of the economic manifestation is Machiavelli's man, Caesar Borgia, or Shakespeare's Iago." [1] Therefore Croce never approves the morality of the Stoics who preached an eternal and immutable justice, but who, at the same time, were dishumanizing human nature and were driving it to despair by pretending that human nature was insensitive to the world of passions. Even Kant aroused in him some doubts—he lamented that Kant's morality was too rigorous. "Moral rigorism has its classical form in Kant, and it is worth mentioning that it falls into vain talk and hypocrisy. The proud and sterile effort of the pure moral will against the passions can

well serve as a symbol of the ethical will and of its
autonomy, but translated into reality this same effort
corrodes itself in the light of facts, in the impossible
struggle and becomes a sort of Stoicism, good if we
want to prepare ourselves for a dignified death, but
not efficacious if we want to live life." [2] When Croce
scolds More, Shaftesbury, La Rochefoucauld and
Mandeville he scolds them because they present morality as harmful and vice as the promoter of progress.
For instance, Mandeville shows that in a society
where no one steals or deceives and where everyone
pays his debts, the judges and the lawyers are con-
demned to inactivity, industrial competition and personal ambition disappear and the society finds itself
doomed to lethargy. On the other hand, wherever
selfishness prevails there is civilization; wherever vice
rules there is progress. For Croce Mandeville's theory
is the wrong defense of the passions. Croce shows enthusiasm toward Vico and Hegel. For Vico the passions are neither good, nor bad, *ex se neque turpes,
neque honestae*,[3] but they are necessary. Without the
world of bestiality there would be no human world.
Because the primitive human beasts had a great sexual
drive they unconsciously gave birth to the institution
of marriage; because the patricians were ambitious
and thirsty for power they founded the city.[4] For
Hegel a passionate person is the person who essentially places the living interest of his spirit, intelligence, character and pleasure on a determinate thing,
and man needs passion in order to accomplish something which is great.

    Economics includes another activity: the legal or
juridical activity. The law is economics. "The juridical activity does not enter into the economic activity: they are both identical. The juridical and the

economic activity are synonymous." [5] Croce is conscious of opposing the entire tradition of the West. In Aristotle justice is a virtue among the virtues. Hegel stresses the very close relationship between law and morality. "Hegel is not interested in the facts of force and violence as the relationship between the slave and the master, facts that belong to the subjective spirit, to a world where violence is still the law. On the contrary, if one encounters violence and tyranny in the field of law this is accidental and it does not alter the nature of the law. In Hegel coercion is born as a reaction to the violation of justice, and its violence is a preservation of freedom and the suppression of the first violence. . . . There is more: the abstract law that constitutes the first moment of Hegel's philosophy of practice is unreal, but its second moment is morality that is also abstract and unreal, a good intention that has not realized itself in action and life. The concrete reality takes place in the third moment that combines the abstract law and the abstract morality of the intention unifying them in social life or ethics." [6] In Schopenhauer the law is reduced to a chapter of the field of ethics; Rosmini considers a legal statute not as a mere eudaemonism but as a eudaemonistic fact which receives its form from the moral law; Trendelenburg views a legal decree as something logical, physical and moral, and therefore he would like to return to the classical tradition of the identification of law with morality; Lasson considers the philosophy of the law as a part of ethics together with the philosophy of custom, the doctrine of the virtues and the theory of the ethical personality. The law is the first of these ethical moments and it refers to man's will as a will still essentially natural. The ethical concept of the law also prevails in Wundt. He thinks of morality as the object of the subjective and objective law. Cohen thinks of the law as the science that systematizes, organizes and writes down *das ungeschriebenes Gesetz,*[7] the eternal unwritten law of morality. It was necessary to destroy the ethical essence of the law. It was necessary to divorce law from morality. In Croce the law becomes economics.

The idea of the economic nature of the law, that is, the law as the *volitive act which has as its content a series or class of actions,* is closely related to some very important concepts. The law is an individual program. Since childhood man begins to legislate within himself, and this interior production continues until death. One will say: I will devote my life to agriculture; another will say: I will concern myself with science. For Croce there is no difference between a man's interior legislation and the social law. The law is free. To the common assertion that individual law is free but social law is compulsory, Croce answers that no law is coercive. Every action is free because the spirit is freedom. Even a terrible despot's order that each of his subjects must sacrifice his firstborn is not coercive. What is the despot to do if man is ready to die for what he believes to be right? Even if the subjects submit themselves to the tyrant they still act freely: they prefer their lives to those of their children. The real law is always the individual law. "It is impossible to divide the law into social and individual law unless we interpret the terms society and individual in an empirical way. By considering the individual in a philosophical way, that is, as the concrete and individualized spirit, it is clear that social laws are individual because in order to observe or to disobey a law it is necessary to make one's own or to expel it from one's personality." [8] The law is unclassifiable. The division of law into juridical, political or social is empirical. If the same concept of social law is empirical, all the distinctions among laws will be empirical. The scientific law is not a law. The scientific law lacks the volitive element. The scientific or natural law is a simple enunciation of the relationships among empirical concepts. The law is not a practical principle. The practical principle has as its object the spirit, a form, a universal, but the law has as its object something material, a class, a product of the spirit. The law is permissive. All laws, whether imperative or prohibitive or permissive, are always permissive: an order is always a prohibition and both orders and prohibitions implicitly allow all the actions that can be the object of the will. "That is to say that outside the law or laws always remains the permissive, the licit, the indifferent, the law or whatever one calls the concept which implies command, prohibition or duty." [9]

Croce continues his analysis. Because the content of law is contingent laws are mutable while the practical principles or laws of universal content are immutable and ready to give form to the most various historical contents. Therefore the impossibility of the Law of Nature. "The Law of Nature, the universal legislation, the eternal code which pretends to immobilize the transient stumbles upon the principle of the mutability of the law which is the necessary consequence of the contingent and historical character of its content." [10]

By the Law of Nature, continues Croce, one has meant a complex of laws that are considered to be better, more rational, more natural than the ancient ones, and for the enthusiasm that they aroused in the heart of man they were thought to be eternal. Everyone knows that in certain times and places religious tolerance, freedom of commerce, private property and constitutional monarchy have been declared to be eternal laws and in other times and places religious intolerance and commercial protectionism have been thought to be above time and place. A residue of the Law of Nature is the doctrine of *natural rights*. "A good morbid residue is the discussion of the *natural rights* of man: a discussion which pretends to establish what *natural rights* and what historical rights belong to man. Among the *natural rights* one finds the right to life, to freedom, to work, to family and so forth; among the historical rights one finds the rights which derive from the constitution of the Italian State or from other special contracts. But outside society (that is, history) no right belongs to man except that of existing as a spirit: a thing that is not a right but a necessary reality." [11]

Another morbid residue of the Law of Nature, adds Croce, is the rejection or the defense of certain institutions not as rational or irrational in the light of historical circumstances but as in harmony or disharmony with the true idea of the Law or with the true idea of those particular institutions. Thus on the one hand one defends women's suffrage, stating that woman is a member of the State; on the other hand one fights it in view of the fact that woman's function is motherhood. On the one hand one proposes divorce because where the harmony of the spirit ceases, there ceases every tie; on the other hand one fights divorce as something contrary to the essence of marriage itself.

Croce criticizes the theory of *natural rights* or *natural institutions* in the light of the contingency of the

law. But Croce is also the philosopher of the concrete-universal, and this fundamental theory makes
him more combative.

For Croce the criterion of judgment or the model
of things is not in a nature above history, in a reason
considered as a pure reason, in the world of ideality,
but it is in the same reality that is the historical and
spiritual reality. For Croce the essence of things is
not separate from the life of men, from the facts that
take place in the course of time, from the texture of
history. Both essence and fact are the same thing.

One can say that Croce understands the nature of
the problem very clearly. For Croce *natural rights* are
not eternal needs, but historical facts, a manifestation
of the necessities of determinate historical periods. For
instance, the same Declaration of the *droits naturels
inaliénables de l'homme* had its importance as a historical fact because it expressed the agreement that
had taken place in the European culture of the
eighteenth century (the age of the *Lumières*) in regard
to the impellent needs of the political reform of European society. And to Huxley who had asked Croce to
give his moral support to UNESCO and to help write
a new Declaration of the *natural rights* Croce an-
swered that UNESCO was a sterile institution and
that the theory of *rights* was philosophically and historically unsound. *Rights* are not outside but within
history.

Was Croce the first thinker to criticize the theory
of *natural rights?* Did this criticism take any special
form during the past centuries? Did he have any
precursor?

Croce's criticism is the product of the long Western tradition. Vico fought against the antihistorical
school of Grotius and Pufendorf; Kant asserted that

liberty is the only inborn and original right because it constitutes man's humanity; [12] Hegel looked upon the *natural rights* as historical categories and Jacobi viewed them as a product of man. For Jacobi virtue is a free art, and as the artistic genius gives laws to art with his works so the moral genius gives laws to moral behaviour: just, good, noble, excellent is what the just, good, noble and excellent man does and produces in conformity with his character. But where Jacobi really anticipates Croce is in the attempt to make Robespierre realize that the "raison," the great reason, which was expected to solve the problems of humanity, was not real reason but real error, a misunderstanding, the abstract intellect; that to conceive a "manière fixe" of government based on pure "raison" was to confuse the reflections derived from experience with the principles that are anterior to every kind of experience; that the real force of history was not the "raisonner" but human concreteness, that is, human feelings.[13]

If the elucidation of the original and profound identification of law with economics is exact, if the exposition of the sameness of both terms is precise, we are more ready to become aware of some other meanings of the category of economics.

Economics is intelligence,[14] but not reason. If reason is the concrete-universal or thought, intelligence is the economic practical activity. While Hegel accepted the abstract intellect as a subordinate degree or moment of reason Croce saw it as a distinct useful activity but not belonging to cognitive activity. But this concept of economics becomes obscure, strange, rigorous in appearance, but arbitrary at every step when it loses its autonomy and becomes the negative: the ugliness in the world of art, evil in the moral field and the error in the realm of logic. "That error that has existence is not error and negativity, but it is something positive, a product of the spirit. Because that product of the spirit is deprived of truth it cannot be the work of the theoretical spirit. Because besides the theoretical form of the spirit there is only the practical form to be considered, the error that we encounter as something existing must be a product of the practical spirit." [15] Croce continues: "He who commits an error has no power to twist, to alter, to corrupt the truth that is his own thought, the thought that operates in him as in everyone, rather as soon as he touches thought he is touched by it too: he thinks and does not err. He only has the practical power to pass from thought to action, and the opening of the mouth or the utterance of sounds to which no thought corresponds is a doing but not a thinking . . . error is a simple economic act." [16]

But even here we should not be misguided by Croce's forceful style. The concept of economics undergoes another change. Economics becomes finite existence. "This last phase of Croce's philosophy is important because it is oriented toward the problems of Existence, problems which are reduced under the general concept of the Vital, and this last phase is accompanied by a polemical but intuitive study of the so-called 'existentialist renaissance of Hegel.' " [17] Economics becomes human existence with the awareness of its sorrow. The old Croce was becoming conscious of his age. One does not find this awareness fully expressed in his pages, but in examining disconnected concepts, tendencies, dislikes, moments of sorrow, continuous "commiati" to Herbart or to others, one securely arrives at this conclusion.

VIII

POLITICS

A thinker who is very interested in the realm of economics or law is bound to face the problem of the State: a problem that affects our daily lives. Therefore Croce took with enthusiasm to the analysis of this problem.

Croce views the State as a spiritual category, but its spirituality is "power," [1] animality, almost nature itself because the State has its own laws which are different from those of the moral world. It can be defined as an immense and perfect animal that satisfies its impulses and needs through wars, struggles, and it is useless to teach it moral lessons because like love it is a *savage oiseau*, of which Carmen sings one *ne peut pas l'apprivoiser*. "The State is the personification of power or animality, and therefore, operating outside the sphere of moral values. As a tiger acts in accordance with its own nature and, therefore, lives outside the world of moral sensibility so the State acts according to its own laws." [2]

The reason why and how Croce conceives the State

as animality can be explained exteriorly by the study of Machiavelli, Hegel and Marx. Machiavelli who conceived the Prince as a centaur, a being that is half man and half animal, Hegel who considered the political genius as a man who is exclusively motivated by the passion of dominion but deprived of an ethical conscience, and Marx who viewed politics as a class struggle had a certain influence upon Benedetto Croce. But more powerful was the Crocian admiration for Vico. A Vico who conceived the State as a phase of the development of the human spirit, the moment of passion that precedes the moment of reason, the moment of animality that precedes the moment of morality had a great impact on Croce. Finally, the Italian cultural tradition was another factor. A Dante who differentiates the sinner's sin from his character, a Galilei who distinguishes religion from science, the inductive from the deductive method, the profane from the divine, a Castiglione who ascertains the specific difference of the gentleman's code from that of the ordinary man and a De Sanctis who expresses the difference between poetry and philosophy constitute the great Italian tradition, the tradition, as says Antoni, of the distinction. While other peoples identified the political with the moral problem, Italy differentiated both problems. Therefore "the hatred toward Machiavelli has become Italophobia and in England the persistent refusal to distinguish between morality and politics has become a constant national trait." [3]

But the concept of this political theory can be explained interiorly by Croce's quality of mind: for him, to think is to distinguish. He characterizes the spirit or reality in four moments: art, philosophy, politics and morality. Positivism which is completely

concerned with the cult of matter does not differentiate art from biology, history from natural science,
the study of society from that of nature: Positivism
believes in the principle of unity. With the concept of
the Idea Hegel himself looks upon the principle of
distinction with horror. The Idea absorbs, unifies and
destroys all differences. Croce, instead, sees a profound
difference between the world of morality and the
realm of politics.

Croce's immense effort in reaffirming the nature
of the State as struggle is expressed in his continuous
difficulties with Anglo-Saxon statesmen who espoused
humanitarian, moralistic and philanthropic ideals
during the First World War; by his continuous in-
sistence upon the torment that he suffered in trying
to defend his political theory in a very hostile world:
a world completely blind to political realism. That
same intense effort was one of the reasons why he felt
himself to be, if not a discoverer, a true assertor of the
concept of politics as animality or power. Neither the
Greeks, nor medieval men, says Croce, had any idea of
this political truth. Plato spoke of the State as a great
human organism, but he never grasped this truth.
Aristotle spoke of the three forms of government:
monarchy, aristocracy and democracy, but he never
intuited the energetic essence of the State. Saint
Thomas and others were also unaware of the true
nature of the political world.

In Treitschke the State is power. Power is the
essential attribute of the State. The State is neither an
economic association, nor a school of belles-lettres, but
it is a society of maximum power, and the individual
has the duty to sacrifice himself to the State: the ideal
of the State is the highest ideal of the human being.
In Croce the State is power but not moral life. While

in Treitschke man lives a moral life only as a member
of the State, in Croce man lives his moral life outside
the State.

But in defending the concept of politics as power
Croce also defends other concepts which are related
to it. Politics is the destruction of utopias. Political
action—party struggles, legislation, conflict over issues,
diplomatic negotiations, trade, treaties, wars—goes
directly against the human ideals of peace, repose and
tranquillity. Politics or State is antiheroic. An individual has the duty to maintain the ideal of human
dignity. He is not allowed to yield to dishonest
threats; he is also forbidden to persist in an error of
which he is aware. On the other hand the State has
no dignity: it does not recognize any error; it does
yield to threats when they are really dangerous.
"What State has kept its dignity in the full ethical
sense of the word during the last war? . . . In the
midst of the struggle one has seen England and the
United States, not conquered but shaken by the
spectacle of German fortune, making peace over-
tures to the arrogant momentary winner who after a
while surrendered with great eagerness and accepted
every order with great docility." [4]

But Croce's political theory, the product of a
powerful mind, seems to oscillate. In the Crocian
political thought there is a contradiction. Croce is
not satisfied with the conception of the State as power
or struggle but he adds that the State is economics.
"Vain is it to try to differentiate political actions
from those which are practical and utilitarian. . . .
What is really the State? It is nothing but a process
of utilitarian actions of a group of individuals." [5]
Therefore Croce defends Machiavelli. In him Croce
reads the confession that it is not possible to judge

a statesman in the light of goodness, loyalty, wicked-
ness and deceit, that is, in terms of virtue and vice.
The same Croce observes that as a painter is judged
as a painter and not as a business man, so the political
man must be judged in the light of economics and not
in view of morality. "The judgment on the statesman
must be technical: the judgment must be on his political skill as one sees in Machiavelli who portrays the
famous Caesar Borgia, the Borgia who appears to him
as the man who can adopt and follow a policy in the
grand manner: a policy which is shrewd, daring and
coherent." [6] Croce recurs to history. History condemns
those who have submitted the interest of the State, to
which they belong as citizens, to an idea, an ideal, a
generous moral duty. For Croce as for Mommsen,
Hannibal and Vercingetorix were wrong in behaving
like "knights"; rather they should always have be-
haved "economically."

Everything pressured Croce toward the economic
nature of the State: his mental participation in the
economic contrasts or conflicts of the Italian South
and his admiration for Labriola, Sorel and Marx. It
is true that Croce criticized Marx strongly. In Marx
he saw the poetical division of humanity into two
groups: the group of the executioners and the group
of the victims; the millennium, that is, the era during
which there will be no struggle, no State, no history,
no necessity for moral law; the attempt to obscure a
truth which is essential to the process of life: resigna-
tion and courage. But Croce also considered Marx as
the assertor of the identification of economics or
"utile economico" with politics.

But Croce was not a blind disciple of Marx. While
in Marx the economic-political element was a material
force now against the spirit, now above the spirit, in

Croce the economic-political element is the spiritual world. While in Marx the economic-political element is pure matter, Croce lifts it to the dignity of an eternal category of the human spirit.

Croce took great pride in having been the first to make this distinction. He felt that he had the courage to have added a new category to the human spirit. "In the course of the centuries the forms and categories of reality and spirit, the supreme values, were divided (*consensu gentium*) into a triad: the true, the good and the beautiful, and it is my opinion that we should integrate this triad with a fourth term, the Economic or the Vital: a term which has been despised, scorned and considered materialistic by the philosophers who did not dare to rebel against the traditional triadic conception."[7]

It is also important to notice that Croce seems to be divided mentally and psychologically before the economic nature of the State: the concept now appears to be a great truth, now it appears to be the awareness of an ugly historical experience. At times he speaks of this concept with reluctance as when he says that a political crime is not crime when it is done for the sacred protection of the State and not for the satisfaction of a private ambition, or as when he looks at the historical figures of Frederick the Great and Cavour and he finds them full of anguish before some terrible political acts. At times he speaks of the economic essence of the State with fervor as when he praises Marx as the firm assertor of the true nature of the world of politics.

At this point a word of caution is necessary. Should the reader view the theory of the State as economics as something definitive he would be mistaken. Croce also speaks of the ethical nature of the

State. "The word 'State' acquires a new meaning: it is not a simple utilitarian relationship, a synthesis of strength and consent, of authority and liberty but is the incarnation of the human ethos, and therefore ethical State or State of Culture as one prefers to say." [8] In Croce the statesman (the manifestation of the State) cannot be a statesman without a moral conscience. As a poet who has no feeling, no thought, no morality is a deficient poet so the statesman who lacks moral sensibility is not a real statesman. A political man who is not moral is incapable of handling men whose psychology he does not know. The contrary is also true. The moral man who removes himself from the political arena in order to live a scholarly life, to enjoy social tranquillity, to live in the countryside becomes sterile. Once one breaks the ties with the political life art, science and agriculture wither, the life of the spirit becomes empty and the effort of generosity, mercy and love weakens in such a way that it loses its effectiveness.

One can say that the Fascists' immoral political atmosphere gave Croce the occasion to grasp the moral essence of the State. "I myself owe a debt of gratitude to Fascism because it gave me a new youth by making me more operose and combative; it forced me to meditate on political problems that I would never have analyzed otherwise; it made me feel that the work of the thinker must blend with that of the man and citizen." [9] Croce became fully aware that a State which disregards moral life associates itself with barbarism. It was necessary to assert the moral essence of the State: a thing that Croce does with fervor.

IX

MORALITY

In the realm of morality as well as in the field of aesthetics Croce firmly opposed the ideas of his time. Against those who were reducing the moral life to the cult of violence as one sees in Nietzsche or to the celebration of sensation as one observes in D'Annunzio Croce espouses a rational morality. Against Pascoli's Arcadian ideal, a world where man sits by the flowing brook and lives in peace with his fellow creatures, Croce upholds Carducci's moral ideal: life as seriousness, action, acceptance of earthly joys and sorrows. But Croce is also connected with the Kantian movement of the eighteenth century. Actually Croce always considered Kant as one of his four spiritual fathers, together with Vico, Hegel and De Sanctis. While Croce satisfied his desire for beauty in Vico and De Sanctis and his philosophical anxiety in Hegel, in Kant he found his moral teacher. I would add that together with Kant Croce also mentions his beloved Herbart though he neglects to mention Her-

der, Novalis and others whose moral motifs are
evident.

The connection is recognized, as I have said, by
Croce himself. It is clear that Croce is not a blind
Kantian disciple; rather he modifies and continues
Kant's ethics. Thus Croce offers some contrasts to
Kant's capital theses, but he also presents himself as
a continuant of Kant's ideas. Kant provided Croce
with the fundamental solution but also with problems: problems that Croce tries to solve in his own
personal way.

Kant's morality was profound, and it is necessary
to clarify it. In the Kantian ethics the categorical imperative was paramount. The categorical imperative
was not heteronomy but autonomy, not dependence
but independence, not exterior but interior law.
"Kant maintains that before him morality was
founded on the heteronomy of the will and that he
has been the first thinker to base it on autonomy.
All other forms of previous ethics, including that of
the Gospel, are reduced by Kant to eudaemonology,
that is, the form of ethics that enforces moral obliga-
tion by its relation to happiness or personal well-
being: with Kant *pure morality* takes place."[1] Not
by chance the idea of the categorical imperative encouraged young Germans to follow a rigid life perspective. Especially after Kant's death the *Critique of
Practical Reason* appeared to Germans what Aristotle's *Ethics* was to the English upper classes during
the past century.

Kant's philosophy finds acceptance in Croce's
spirit. Kant's moral autonomy becomes the volition of
the universal, freedom, reality. Morality ceases to be
the obedience to a supreme being or particular interests in order to become the cult of reality, progress,

civilization, spirit itself. "What is the requirement which gives a moral character to action? It is nothing but the law that rules the world, the law of the perpetual self-growth of the world. Man, every man, each man, each one according to his own way, actively participates in this process. In this process participates the poet who with his poetical creation makes a new chord of the soul palpitate or a new palpitation of the universe vibrate; in this process participates the philosopher who with his concept amplifies and invigorates the power of thought in order to penetrate into the reality of events." [2] Croce continues: "All the forms of spiritual activity promote life with their works of truth, beauty and utility. Because of these works reality is contemplated and understood, the land is covered with tilled fields and factories, families are formed, States are founded, one fights, one sheds his blood, one wins and progresses. What does morality add to these beautiful, true and variously useful works? One will say: good works. But actually good works are nothing but the works of beauty, truth, utility. In order to realize itself morality itself becomes passion, will and utility: it thinks with the philosopher; it molds with the artist; it labors with the farmer and the worker; it gives birth to children, adopts policies, makes war and makes use of the hand and the sword." [3]

But Croce's Kantism becomes more apparent and almost dramatic in his struggle against utilitarianism. Let us clarify this important point.

The two important representatives of utilitarianism whom Croce often mentions are Bentham and Adam Smith though at times he does not neglect the names of Hartley, Hume, Warburton, Paley and others. Croce condemns Bentham very strongly. Ben-

tham, says Croce, reduces the moral world to the
quantitive calculation of pleasures. Croce admires
Smith's enthusiasm for the world of economics, but
he also condemns him for his ethical utilitarianism.
The utilitarian doctrine appears to Croce to be the
doctrine of those who have no faith in the spirituality
of man: a being who only lives in order to satisfy
his own selfish needs. Severe also is Croce's opinion in
regard to the general ethics of the last part of the
nineteenth century: an ethics now based on the idea
of compassion and on the five practical ideas as one
observes in Schopenhauer and Herbart; now based on
love and benevolence as one sees in Feuerbach and
Lotze; now based on theology and life as one notices
in Baader and Nietzsche. For similar reasons Croce
could not be satisfied with the traditional versions of
morality: morality now as altruism, now as social
service, now as the obedience of God's will. In al-
truistic morality Croce finds that a blind and irrational attachment to others is ultimately an "attachment to ourselves, to our nerves, to our fantasies, to
our comforts, to our habits. This is utilitarianism, but
not morality because morality wants us to be ready to
detach us from ourselves as well as from others and
wants us to leave wife, sons and brothers in order to
follow duty: a duty that transcends everything." [4] In
social morality Croce finds that society, State and
other institutions do not express the universality of
reality but only a group of particular manifestations:
the life that is called social or political. The moral
man, instead, always defends and helps to develop
certain attitudes of the human species: he always
serves the ideal but not the historical interests. In
religious morality Croce finds that morality becomes

an attachment to a supreme being and this attachment is always based on love or fear.

Not only the Kantian concept of moral autonomy is espoused by Croce but also another fundamental Kantian theory: the universality of the moral world.[5] Man is an animal, a being with ferocious instincts, an entity in whom the presence of the "economic" is evident. Man fights, destroys and at times he is the "anti-Christ" himself. Will humanity survive its own animality? Though man is an animal, he always has, says Croce, the spark of moral conscience. "Not even anthropophagy is immoral, irrational or unnatural because the anthropophagites (though the thing is repugnant to our hearts and to our stomachs as civilized Europeans) were men who felt themselves to be very honest, and nevertheless they ate a fellow creature with the same tranquillity with which we eat a roasted chicken without any hatred toward the chicken because we know that we cannot do otherwise."[6] Croce comes close to Vico. For Vico the primitive human beasts cover the earth with altars, have sexual intercourse in caves and bury the dead because they have the *timor Dei*. "Col conato altresí incominciò in essi a spuntare la virtú dell'animo, contenendo la loro libidine bestiale di esercitarla in faccia al cielo, di cui avevano uno spavento grandissimo; e ciascuno di essi si diede a trascinare per sé una donna dentro le grotte e tenerlavi dentro in perpetua compagnia di loro vita."[7]

But our purpose is not only to expound Croce's Kantism but also his opposition to Kant, and especially his criticism of Kant's implicit or explicit dualisms: the dualism between intention and volition, volition and action, good and evil, necessary and free action, morality and moral precepts. Croce identifies intention with volition. The identification of intention with volition, says Croce, is not only a matter of good sense but is also the basis of the realistic doctrine of the will. A real intention always translates itself into a volition.[8] To those who oppose the abstract to the concrete and affirm that one wants the good in an abstract and not in a concrete way, and therefore one can have a good intention and can still behave badly, Croce answers that to want in an abstract way is not to want anything because a volition always requires a certain determinate historical situation from which it originates as a determinate and concrete act. Croce identifies volition with action. There is no real action which is not an act of the will, and there is no act of the will which does not manifest itself in an action. "No positive manifestation of the will, even though it is not translated into what we usually call external act or action, lacks realization: at least it has realization in us, getting us ready for certain moods which, in their turn, produce certain effects." [9] Croce identifies the good with the evil action, or in Kant's terminology, the two "categories of freedom." [10] For Croce every real action, as far as an action, considered in itself as adequate to its particular end, is good. If one substitutes to that end another, the first end will appear as evil, and the second as good; but if this substitution takes place before the action, then the action is inevitably directed towards the second end, and therefore again, it is not evil but good. "Old is the observation that everyone looks after his own good and no man wants his own evil, and if the wise man is the learned man, the wicked can only be the ignorant." [11] For Croce the volitive act is free and necessary. Every act of the will is free because it always produces something different, new, something which did not exist before. Every act of the will is necessary because it is conditioned by a certain situation. "True poet is he who feels himself related to his predecessors and free, determined and free like Homer, Dante and Shakespeare who reflect centuries of history, thought and poetry and who also add something to their previous tradition." [12] Croce abolishes the dualism between morality and moral norms. It is not possible, says Croce, to supply models or fixed types of action: he who seeks and waits for these models and types is an individual who does not know how to want and is deprived of initiative, of that creativity that is as indispensable to practical activity as it is indispensable to art and philosophy.

It is easy to find the precedent for this doctrine. For Goethe the ethical man does not have before him a system of precepts, a table of commandments but he has before him a principle that is the vital impulse. *"Denn es ist Drang, und so ist's Pflicht."* "If we want to force Croce's ethics into a formula one can say that to the traditional scheme—the moral *act,* the moral *norm,* the supreme *principle* of the good—Croce replaces the immediate combination of the principle and of the act and he abolishes the conjunctive ring, the mediative element of the norm. The moral act translates the universal principle into concreteness and in free autonomy does not bind itself to prefixed precepts, that is, a casuistic 'authorized system.' " [13]

Croce gives an original interpretation of the ethical problem. Nevertheless he compromises the fundamental postulate of the moral world: man's individuality. It is true that Croce recognizes the value of man's individuality in his critical analysis of Italian and foreign poets: an analysis in which Croce distinguishes the artist's soul from the social milieu in which he lives and dies; that Croce accentuates man's dramatic feeling of life in difficult situations where he must decide whether to follow his moral conscience or the legal code; that Croce emphasizes the thinker's personal struggle in the world of thought as one sees in his essay on Hegel; that Croce himself feels the dignity of man when he opposes Mussolini's regime. In spite of this, Croce's philosophy appears to weaken the idea of man's individuality: freedom, spirituality, uniqueness. Croce says that man is the manifestation of the universal: in the *Storia d'Europa nel secolo decimonono* Mazzini and Cavour are treated more as ideas than as men, more as the instruments of the eternal than as historical persons and Italian liberalism itself seems to lose its national color before the oceanic expanse of the "new religion" of liberty. Croce asserts that man is the complex of "inborn attitudes, dispositions and tendencies." [14] A poet who forces himself to be a tailor will never be a good tailor; a woman who coerces herself to be a mathematician will be a superficial one; an industrialist who wants to be a saint or a hero will live a moral life without enthusiasm. Behind Croce's celebration of the natural tendencies one can almost perceive a certain determinism. Croce affirms that man is an "institution"; [15] that man consists of two entities: the "empirical" and the "ideal" one; that "the person is never found in the world of historical thought because he is foreign to the pure truth and belongs to another world: the practical world." [16] In these definitions of man one finds concepts which are irreconcilable with the central postulate of the ethical world:

man's individuality. Croce can actually be considered
as the assertor of spiritualism and determinism.

But if in the field of morality Croce is a theorist,
he also appears to be a great psychologist though he
never had any respect for this discipline. The reader
finds some very keen observations. For Croce remorse
does not indicate the presence of a good moral conscience: even a wicked man repents not having been
more destructive. For Croce self-discovery is very
difficult. "The first duty of every individual who wants
to operate effectively consists in the search for his self,
in the examination of his own dispositions, in the
verification of the quality of the attitudes that
Reality has deposited in him at the moment of his
birth as well as during his lifetime: he must know
his attitudes or passions not to destroy them but in
order to develop them. The search is not easy, and in
this search one spends the preparatory period of life:
youth." [17] Croce reflects on human psychology. For
him there are three psychological types: the fantastic
man, that is, the man who easily makes plans and
projects and then never realizes them; the perplexed
and fearful type who never starts anything because
his mind is crowded with the phantasms of possible
failure, and because the possibility of failure is infinite, he goes from one fear to another and never
decides to operate; the type who is broken by the
misfortunes of the past and, as such, unable to live
the present. For Croce the first type lacks concreteness,
the second courage, the third love of life. All three
types lack the volitive strength, that is, concreteness,
courage, love of life. What do they have in exchange?
They have nothing, and this is the evil, the reason
for their anxiety. Croce meditates on the concept of
perfection. Unfortunate is the person who does not

feel the stimulus of perfection that is the same stimulus of doing, of a doing trying to achieve its purpose,
of *perficere,* but more unfortunate is the person who
tries to realize, to personify, to materialize perfection
itself. This person converts a beneficial and fecund
tendency, a great spiritual law into a sterile sadness
and fixation, a true life into a paralysis. "Powerful
and genuine artists, scientists, industrious people, men
worthy of the name do not run after these phobias,
and if they look for perfection they fear imperfection
but not excessively. They feel that the main problem,
though at times they are not fully aware of it, is not
to overwin but to win, to tame the adversary but not
to kill him." [18] But we want to abstain from accenting
Croce's psychological insights. That is not the purpose
of this book. But we do want to add that Croce was
a theoretical philosopher but also a man whose
human perception was discerning, perspicacious and
acute.

X

THE LAST YEARS

An old man is always nostalgic about the past, but this is not Croce's case. He never attempted to escape from the historical present, and if at times he expressed a longing for the Italy of Carducci, Spaventa, De Sanctis and Labriola, the time when Italy had a great intellectual vigor, this was a simple nostalgia, a moment of spiritual fatigue, but not an indication of his true attitude. This nostalgia for the past was also the result of a specific historical circumstance. A man who sees himself immersed in the tragedy of the Second World War and who sees the lack of international comprehension of the Italian political problem was certainly encouraged to poetize the past.

I want now to comment on Croce's teaching and other interior qualities: charity, patriotism and courage.

Croce was not the old university teacher. The traditional Italian teacher or literary man loved more letters than art, that is, he loved more literature than poetry, more the words than the style and, says Croce, more the parts than the aesthetic organism. If he was indifferent to art, he was also adverse to the profound study of philosophy and history or the political or religious life of the people. He was incapable of feeling the spiritual or cultural storms. On the other hand, Croce was open to the currents and crosscurrents of modern intellectual life. The great psychological experiences that his long life had deposited in his soul and his love for teaching also contributed to make him a great teacher.

In contrast to the selfishness of many wealthy Italians, a selfishness that is the main stain on Italian society, Croce was very generous. Now he was helping a friend in need; now he was paying a poor student's tuition. "If many times Croce stubbornly refused to write a recommendation letter, a thing that seemed to him to be very indelicate, many times he paid the tuition for promising students. He also helped young authors to publish their first books almost at his own expense. Some needy friends would not have overcome difficult moments if Croce had not instructed Giovanni Laterza to give them a double or triple price for their translations or other works." [1] But Croce's charity was also extended to his enemies as can be seen in this noble passage from his diary. "April 17, 1944. Early this morning the good Brindisi has come to Capri to discuss with me what he is doing, and in the middle of the conversation he told me that on the boat he had heard that Gentile had been murdered in Florence! . . . This past August I was displeased by a letter of reproach that the new Minister of Education had directed to Gentile and I recommended that he proceed toward him with temperance and I encouraged a mutual friend to advise him to anticipate his retirement with a spontaneous request. . . . Then happened what happened: Italy was split in two. . . ." [2]

Croce was a patriot. To an Italy divided into two political entities, partially destroyed by foreign soldiers and completely disoriented in a world completely hostile, Croce gave superb encouragement. During those difficult years he published the famous essay *Perchè non possiamo non dirci "cristiani."* In this essay Croce presented Christianity as the greatest world revolution: a revolution which was so immense, so profound, so pregnant with the future of the world: a revolution in the light of which all the other revolutions appear limited, narrow, provincial. But in this same essay Croce also interprets Christianity as the source of the moral and civil life of a people, a source which the Italians were encouraged to cultivate in order to overcome the crisis of the present.

It is hard to judge the amount of physical suffering that Croce had to endure in the last year of his life, but one thing is certain: Croce died with courage. "At times to my friends who ask me the usual question: 'How are you?' I answer with the same words that Salvatore Di Giacomo heard from the dying old Duke of Maddaloni, the famous Neapolitan epigrammatist: 'Don't you see? I am dying.' This is not a lament which comes out of my heart, but it is a reminiscence of one of the usual literary anecdotes that curiously return to my mind—anecdotes that give me joy. Though death is sad and melancholic I am too much of a philosopher not to see clearly that it would be terrible were man never to die, were man forever shut up in the prison that is life. . . . Now the entire life is a preparation for death and there is nothing to do except to continue life and to perform all the duties that are necessary." [3] For Croce life interweaves with death and both life and death constitute the indivisible whole, the indivisible life that is the spiritual life of the universe.

Chapter I Notes

1, 2. Giovanni Castellano, *Introduzione allo studio delle opere di B. Croce* (Bari, 1920), pp. 250-251.

3. Ibid., p. 253.

4. Ibid., p. 261.

5. Guido Calogero, "Benedetto Croce," *The Atlantic*, Vol. 202, No. 6, 1959, p. 132.

6. Croce, *Terze pagine sparse* (Bari, 1955), Vol. II, p. 209.

7. Croce, *Indagini su Hegel* (Bari, 1952), p. 3.

8. Ibid., p. 75.

Chapter II Notes

1. Taine, *Philosophie de l'art* (Paris, 1917), Pr. I, p. 13.

2. Xavier León, *La philosophie de Fichte* (Paris, 1902), pp. 20-25.

3. Hegel, *System und Geschichte der Philosophie* (Leipzig, 1940), pp. 97-99.

4. Hegel, *Enciclopädie*, Par. 244.

5. Croce, *Logica come scienza del concetto puro* (Bari, 1928), p. 110. I want to add that Croce did not elaborate his monistic spiritualism until 1909. Before this time he was an idealist, but he still was a little dualistic. "Outside the intuitions or representations there are only impressions, sensations, feelings, impulses, emotions, or whatever is called what is still outside the spirit." Croce, *Estetica* (Bari, 1909), p. 14.

6. Ibid., pp. 3, 63.

7. Calogero, "Benedetto Croce," *The Atlantic,* op. cit., p. 131.

8. Croce, *Cultura e vita morale* (Bari, 1926), p. 44. I want to recall a Comte passage. "Je n'ai jamais lu, en aucune langue, ni Vico, ni Kant, ni Herder, ni Hegel, etc.; je ne connais leurs divers ouvrages que d'après quelques relations indirectes et certains ex-

traits fort insuffisants. Quels que puissent être les inconvénients réeles de cette négligence volontaire, je suis convaincu qu'elle a beaucoup contribué à la pureté et a l'harmonie de la philosophie sociale." A. Comte, *Cours de philosophie positive* (Paris, 1908), Tome VI, Préface personelle, p. XXVI.

9. Croce, *Estetica,* op, cit., p. 36.

10. Bergson, *"Introduction à la Métaphysique,"* *Revue de métaphysique et de morale,* Vol. XI, p. 29.

11. "Aber unsere Gedanken, unsere Erwartungen, richten sich nach anderen Gedanken, nach den Begriffen nämlich, welche wir uns von den Tatsachen gebildet haben." Mach, *Erkenntnis und Irrtum* (Leipzig, 1905), p. 448.

Chapter III Notes

1. A very small portion of this and the following chapter appeared in my article "The Drama of the Aesthetics of Benedetto Croce," *The Journal of Aesthetics and Art Criticism*, Vol. XV, pp. 117-121.

2. Croce, *Estetica*, op. cit., p. 12.

3. Croce, *Nuovi saggi di estetica* (Bari, 1926), p. 10.

4. Ibid., p. 11.

5. Ibid., p. 13.

6. Ibid., pp. 15-16.

7. Croce, *Estetica*, op. cit., p. 133.

8. Ibid., p. 78.

9. Croce, *Estetica*, op. cit., p. 139.

10. Ibid., p. 156.

11. Ibid., p. 115.

12. Croce, *Saggio sullo Hegel* (Bari, 1948), pp. 83-84.

13. Croce, *Estetica*, op. cit., p. 170.

14. Ibid., p. 76.

15. Croce, *Nuovi saggi di estetica*, op. cit., p. 122.

16. Croce, *Saggio sullo Hegel* (Bari, 1927), p. 37.

17. Croce, *Ultimi saggi* (Bari, 1935), p. 10.

18. Ibid., p. 11.

19. Croce, *La poesia* (Bari, 1946), p. 9.

20. Croce, *Discorsi di varia filosofia* (Bari, 1945), Vol. II, p. 87.

21, 22. Croce, *La poesia,* op. cit., p. 34.

23. Croce, *Filosofia della pratica* (Bari, 1923), p. 172.

24. Croce, *Storia dell'età barocca in Italia* (Bari, 1929), p. 238.

25. "Die Wünsche, die sich im härteren Medium der Realität nicht durchsetzen konnten, kommen in diesem irdischen Jenseits zu bescheidener Erfüllung. Zwei Begierden werden besonders ausgezeichnet: die erotischen und die ehrgeizen. Eine Generation vor Freud zeichnete auch Balzac sie aus: in der 'Comedie Humaine.'" Ludwig Marcuse, "Freud's Aesthetik," *PMLA,* Vol. LXXII, p. 448.

26. Croce, *Estetica,* op. cit., p. 24.

27. Croce, *Nuovi saggi,* op, cit., p. 152. We also want to add that Croce is for art-intuition from 1900 to 1912; for art-universality from 1912 to 1928; for art-morality from 1928 to 1936; for art-poetic expression from 1936 until his death in 1952. It is understood that these dates are only approximate, but they do give the idea of change.

Chapter IV Notes

1. Sainte-Beuve, *Étude sur Virgile* (Paris, 1883), pp. 88-89.

2. Croce, *La letteratura della nuova Italia* (Bari, 1949), Vol. III, p. 306.

3. Hegel, *The Philosophy of Fine Art,* trans. Osmaston (London, 1920), Vol. I, p. 77.

4. Croce, *La letteratura,* op. cit., p. 33.

5. Ibid., pp. 147-148.

6. Croce, *Goethe* (Bari, 1959), Vol. I, p. 9.

7. Croce, *La poesia di Dante* (Bari, 1922), p. 82.

8. Croce, *Ariosto* (Bari, 1927), p. 47.

9. Ibid., pp. 63-64.

10. Croce, *Storia dell'età barocca,* op. cit., p. 237.

11. Ibid., p. 237.

12. Croce, *Poesia antica e moderna* (Bari, 1950), pp. 35-36.

Chapter V Notes

1. Croce, *Saggio sullo Hegel,* op. cit., p. 15.
2. Croce, *Logica come scienza del concetto puro* (Bari, 1928), p. 17.
3. Croce, *Saggio sullo Hegel,* op. cit., p. 15.
4. Windelband, *Storia della filosofia moderna* (Firenze, 1942), Vol. I, p. 123.
5. Bruno, *De la causa principio e uno* in *Dialoghi metafisici* (Bari, 1907), p. 257.
6. Croce, *Saggio sullo Hegel,* op. cit., p. 39.
7. Croce, *Logica,* op. cit., p. 137.
8. Croce, *Logica,* op. cit., p. 200.
9. "La mentalité primitive, comme la nôtre, s'inquiète des causes de ce qui arrive. Mais elle ne les cherche pas dans la même direction. Elle vit dans un monde où d'innombrables puissances occultes, partout présentes, sont toujours ou agissantes ou prêtes de agir. . . . Pour des esprits aussi orientés, il n'y a pas de fait purement physique. Aucune question relative aux phénomènes de la nature on se pose donc pour eux comme pour nous." Lévy-Bruhl, *La mentalité primitive* (Paris, 1925), pp. 510, 512.

10. Croce, *Logica,* op. cit., p. 115.

11. Spencer, *First Principles* (New York, 1910), p. 367.

12. Croce, *Il carattere della filosofia moderna* (Bari, 1945), p. 195.

Chapter VI Notes

1. Croce, *Estetica*, op. cit., p. 32.
2. Vico, *La scienza nuova seconda* (Bari, 1942), Pr. I, p. 148.
3. Croce, *Teoria e storia della storiografia* (Bari, 1927), p. 74.
4. See my article "Benedetto Croce e Charles Austin Beard," *Italica*, Vol. XXXV, pp. 112-118.
5. Charles A. Beard, "Written History as an Act of Faith," *The American Historical Review*, Vol. XXXIX, p. 220. Croce and Beard also come close to Droysen. For Droysen the historical narration is neither a photography, nor a deposit of news, but the subjective exposition of one's point of view. In opposition to Ranke Droysen calls "objectivity" the "objectivity of the eunuchs." "Gli basta la verità relativa al suo punto di vista, assicuratogli dalla sua patria, dalla sua convinzione politica e religiosa, dal suo serio studio: bisogna avere il coraggio, egli dichiara alla fine del corso, di riconoscere questo limite, consolandoci col fatto che il limitato è più ricco e vivo dell'universale." Carlo Antoni, *Considerazioni su Hegel e Marx* (Napoli, 1946), p. 123.
6. Croce, *Teoria e storia*, op. cit., p. 177.

7. Croce, *Critica,* No. 4, 1912, p. 303.

8. Croce, *Storia come pensiero e come azione* (Bari, 1954), p. 6.

9. Quoted by Croce, *Etica e politica* (Bari, 1956), p. 288.

10. See my article "The Concept of Art in Adriano Tilgher," *The Journal of Aesthetics and Art Criticism,* Vol. XVII, pp. 457-462.

11. "The great theme of Pareto was the identification of ideologies with 'derivations.' The world of social facts is obscured by a thick cloud of reasonings or fragments of reasonings that men create in order to give an appearance of logic to their fundamental instincts (the so-called 'residues'). He who gives importance to the study of the derivations and neglects the residues . . . mistakes the accident for the substance and adds confusion to confusion." *La filosofia contemporanea in Italia* (Roma, 1948), Vol. I, p. 341.

12. Croce, *Il carattere della filosofia,* op. cit., p. 35.

13. Croce, *Storia dell'età,* op. cit., p. 474.

14. Croce, *Storia d'Italia dal 1871 al 1915* (Bari, 1943), p. 179.

15. Croce, *Storia dell'età barocca,* op. cit., p. 10.

16. Croce, *Discorsi di varia filosofia* (Bari, 1945), Vol. II, p. 193.

17. Croce, *Indagini su Hegel,* op. cit., pp. 5-6.

18. Croce, *Saggio sullo Hegel* (Bari, 1948), p. 42.

Chapter VII Notes

1. Croce, *Estetica,* op. cit., pp. 65-66.
2. Croce, *Etica e politica,* op. cit., p. 98.
3. Vico, *De uno universalis juris principio,* Par. 36.
4. Vico, *La scienza,* op. cit., p. 250.
5. Croce, *Filosofia della pratica* (Bari, 1923), p. 370.
6. Croce, *Filosofia della pratica* (Bari, 1957), p. 379.
7. Cohen, *Ethik des reinen Willens* (Berlin, 1904), p. 248.
8. Croce, *Filosofia della pratica* (Bari, 1923), pp. 330-331.
9. Croce, *Filosofia della pratica* (Bari, 1957), p. 334.
10. Croce, *Filosofia della pratica* (Bari, 1923), p. 323.
11. Ibid., p. 343.
12. Kant, *Metaphysik der Sitten* (1797), ed. Kirchmann, p. 40.
13. Jacobi, *Werke* (Leipzig, 1910), Vol. II, p. 544.
14. Croce, *Logica* op. cit., p. 228.
15. Croce, *Logica come scienza del concetto puro* (Bari, 1958), p. 254.
16. Ibid., pp. 254-256.
17. Raffaello Franchini, *Metafisica e storia* (Napoli, 1958), pp. 118-119.

Chapter VIII Notes

1. Croce, *Materialismo storico ed economia marx-istica* (Bari, 1917), Prefazione.

2. See my article "An Approach to Benedetto Croce," *The Personalist.* Vol. XLII, No. 1.

3. Carlo Antoni, *Commento a Croce* (Venezia, 1955), p. 20.

4. Croce, *Etica e politica,* op. cit., pp. 180-181.

5. Croce, *Elementi di politica* (Bari, 1946), pp. 10-11.

6. Croce, *Discorsi,* op. cit., p. 215.

7. Croce, *Filosofia e storiografia* (Bari, 1949), p. 17.

8. Croce, *Elementi,* op. cit., p. 28.

9. Croce, *Terze pagine,* op. cit., Vol. I, p. 116.

Chapter IX Notes

1. Francesco Fiorentino, *Manuale di storia della filosofia* (Perugia, 1929), p. 278.

2. Croce, *Filosofia e storiografia,* op. cit. p. 169.

3. Croce, *La storia come pensiero,* op. cit., p. 44.

4. Croce, *Filosofia della pratica* (Bari, 1923), p. 283.

5. "It is the case to recall how in the *Introduction* to the *Metaphysical Elements of the Doctrine of Virtue* (XII) Kant observes that there are certain conditions which, though they do not constitute the foundation of morality, are the subjective conditions which incline man to the idea of duty, conditions whereby man is capable of being obliged. A duty to procure these conditions cannot exist, says Kant, (evidently if we did not have them we could never acquire them), but these conditions, he adds, exist in every man.

"How do they exist? The most important conditions are moral feeling and conscience . . . and Kant adds: 'There is no man deprived of moral feeling, because if man were deprived of this feeling he could not exist morally . . . conscience is not something that one acquires, and there is no duty that prescribes its procurement, but every man, as a moral man, has it within himself originally.' " Giuseppe Rensi, *Il genio etico* (Bari, 1912), pp. 177-178.

6. Croce, *Filosofia della pratica*, op. cit., p. 326.

7. Vico, *La scienza nuova seconda* (Bari, 1942), Part I, p. 218.

8. Croce wavers over the relationship between theoretical and practical activity. "Without will knowledge is thinkable but will which is independent from knowledge is unthinkable. A blind will is not a will; will must have eyes." *Estetica,* op. cit., p. 56. "Practical activity is thought that realizes itself." *Filosofia della pratica* (Bari, 1957), p. 13. "The primacy that one holds here is not the primacy of a particular form of the spirit over others, but the primacy of the principle which rules over all the single forms. This principle is action: the activity against the passivity of contemplation." *Filosofia e storiografia,* op. cit., p. 5.

9. Croce, *Frammenti di etica* (Bari, 1922), p. 12.

10. Kant, *Kritik der praktischen Vernunft,* ed. Kirchmann, p. 79.

11. Croce, *Filosofia della pratica* (Bari, 1923), p. 130.

12. Ibid., p. 115.

13. *Benedetto Croce a cura di Francesco Flora* (Napoli, 1953), p. 175. Bergson states the same thing. "For Bergson the conventional and static morality is the product of utilitarianism, but morality is the product of the soul in motion, inspiration, enthusiasm. According to this thinker the universe is animated by a creative energy that discharges itself into the inert matter and seeks to vivify it. Matter fights back and stops the vital current, crystallizes it in the different living species. . . . There is a static, selfish,

utilitarian, simple morality that corresponds to the crystallized part of humanity. . . . There is a dynamic morality or religion that tends to break the closed circle of nature, the small group, the suffocating society, the narrow-minded nationalisms in order to spread itself to the whole of humanity." Giuseppe Rensi, *La morale come pazzia* (Modena, 1942), pp. 228-229.

14. Croce, *Filosofia della pratica,* op. cit., p. 151.
15. Croce, *Frammenti,* op. cit., p. 95.
16. Croce, *Discorsi,* op. cit., Vol. II, p. 147.
17. Croce, *Filosofia della pratica,* op. cit., p. 153.
18. Croce, *Etica e politica,* op. cit., p. 140.

Chapter X Notes

1. *Benedetto Croce a cura,* op. cit., p. 168.
2. Ibid., p. 172.
3. Croce, *Terze pagine,* op. cit., p. 119.

NAME INDEX